COMET-X MEDIA

QUESTIONS TO WHICH
NO ONE KNOWS
THE ANSWERS

DUSTIN MALONE

COMET-X MEDIA

The most creative people are willing to tolerate a certain amount of chaos and disorder—and even to relish it—as the cost of pushing beyond the obvious. They're willing to ask 'stupid' questions, and they're willing to be wrong.

Warren Berger

BY DUSTIN MALONE

FOREWORD

In the grand expanse of human knowledge, there exists a captivating realm where questions linger without clear answers, akin to undiscovered treasures waiting to be unearthed. Imagine embarking on a thrilling expedition, armed not with maps but with a boundless curiosity that propels you into the uncharted territories of the mind. "Questions No One Knows the Answers To" beckons you to join this expedition, a literary voyage into the enigmatic corners of our understanding.

Picture this book as a compass guiding you through the unexplored territories of what we haven't quite figured out yet. It's not just about the unknown; it's about the mysteries that make us pause and ponder, igniting that insatiable curiosity that defines us as seekers of knowledge. Why does this matter, you ask? Because, my friend, curiosity is the spark that has ignited the most extraordinary human discoveries.

As you flip through the pages, each one unfolds like a treasure map leading to a question that challenges the boundaries of what we think we know. Ever wondered why certain things happen or what secrets the universe holds? This book is your ticket to a captivating adventure where each chapter unravels a puzzle, and every paragraph is a step deeper into the mysteries that make us marvel at the wonders of existence.

This isn't just a book; it's an open invitation to be part of a journey where the thrill lies in the pursuit of understanding. It celebrates the beauty of questions that don't have easy answers, inviting you to indulge your curiosity

QUESTION 1

Is time travel possible within the laws of physics?

Once upon a time, scientists were intrigued by the prospect of time travel and wondered if it could align with the rules governing our universe. Their journey into this captivating realm began with the groundbreaking work of a brilliant scientist named Albert Einstein, who introduced the theory of relativity. According to this theory, time is not a constant for everyone everywhere; its flow can either speed up or slow down depending on factors like how fast one is moving or the strength of gravity in their vicinity. In the early stages of their exploration, scientists discovered a phenomenon known as time dilation, a consequence of Einstein's theory. To understand this, they envisioned a scenario where one had a twin, and while one twin embarked on a high-speed space journey, the other stayed on Earth. When the space-traveling twin returned, they found that less time had passed for them compared to their Earthbound sibling. Time dilation, proven through experiments involving high-speed particles and ultra-precise clocks, opened a window into the concept of traveling "into the future." However, as scientists pondered the idea of traveling backward in time, they encountered more complexity. While certain theories hinted at the potential for time travel under specific conditions – like traveling near the speed of light or manipulating gravity – the concept of going back to the past remained elusive. The introduction of wormholes, cosmic shortcuts that could connect different points in spacetime, added a layer of intrigue. Yet, for these to be relevant for time travel, they might require a mysterious substance known as "exotic matter" with peculiar properties, an element that has not been observed or understood. As the story unfolded, scientists faced a conundrum. Some theories suggested that even if time travel were possible, it might lead to paradoxes, such as going back in time and inadvertently preventing one's own existence. This raised profound questions about whether the laws of physics would permit such scenarios or if there were yet-to-be-discovered principles at play.In conclusion, the scientists' journey so far has presented them with fascinating possibilities and tantalizing theories. While time travel into the future has found support within the realms of science, the prospect of traveling back in time remains a mysterious adventure. The pursuit of understanding time and its secrets continues, with scientists delving into the unknown, eager to unlock the next chapters of this captivating tale.

QUESTION 2

What existed before the Big Bang?

Once upon a time, scientists embarked on a quest to unravel the mystery of what existed before the Big Bang, the colossal explosion that marked the beginning of our universe. Their journey began with the understanding that the universe we know today wasn't always here, but rather, it emerged from an incredibly hot and dense state approximately 13.8 billion years ago.

As scientists delved into the cosmic archives, they encountered the challenge of peering beyond the cosmic veil that shrouded the moments before the Big Bang. The laws of physics, as we currently know them, struggle to describe the conditions at that extreme point in time. This sparked curiosity about what might have triggered this cosmic event and what, if anything, existed in the vast cosmic landscape before the grand explosion.

One avenue of exploration led scientists to the concept of a singularity—an infinitesimally small and dense point where all the matter and energy in the universe are concentrated. However, delving into the singularity proved challenging because our understanding of physics breaks down under such extreme conditions.

Another idea that unfolded in their cosmic journey was the notion of cosmic inflation. This proposed that, in the tiniest fraction of a second after the Big Bang, the universe expanded at an astonishing rate, smoothing out irregularities and setting the stage for the structures we observe today. However, the precise origin and cause of this inflationary process remained an enigma.

As the scientists continued their quest, they explored theories that suggested our universe might be just one in a vast multiverse—a collection of countless universes, each with its own unique properties. This idea introduced the possibility that our universe's birth was part of a broader cosmic tapestry.

In the end, the journey to uncover what existed before the Big Bang remains a challenge, as the secrets of that primordial moment are shrouded in the cosmic mists of time. The scientists, armed with powerful telescopes, particle accelerators, and theoretical frameworks, continue their quest, driven by the desire to unlock the cosmic origins and to reveal the cosmic narrative that predates our universe's spectacular beginning. And so, the cosmic tale of exploration and discovery continues, with each discovery bringing us closer to understanding the cosmic dawn that set the stage for the grand cosmic spectacle we witness today.

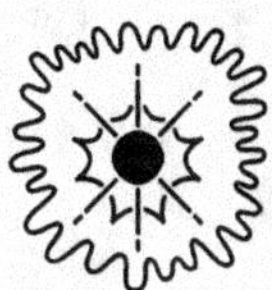

QUESTION 3

Can every even integer greater than 2 be expressed as the sum of two prime numbers, as conjectured by the Goldbach Conjecture?

Once upon a time, mathematicians were intrigued by a puzzle known as the Goldbach Conjecture. This mathematical riddle proposed that every even number greater than 2 could be expressed as the sum of two prime numbers. To unravel this mystery, the mathematicians set out on a journey of exploration.

Their adventure began with the basics of numbers – primes, which are like the building blocks of the numerical world. Primes are special because they can only be divided evenly by 1 and themselves, like 2, 3, 5, and so on. The mathematicians wondered: Could every even number greater than 2 be broken down into the sum of two of these prime numbers?

As the mathematicians delved into the mathematical landscape, they started testing the conjecture with various even numbers. They found that many even numbers could indeed be expressed as the sum of two primes, providing evidence that the Goldbach Conjecture might hold true.

To illustrate, they discovered that 4 is the sum of 2 and 2, 6 is the sum of 3 and 3, 8 is the sum of 3 and 5, and so on. As they journeyed through larger numbers, they found more examples supporting the conjecture.

However, despite their efforts and numerous examples, the mathematicians couldn't definitively prove that the Goldbach Conjecture held true for all even numbers. The challenge lay in demonstrating that the pattern they observed would persist indefinitely for every even number.

Over time, the mathematicians devised clever strategies and algorithms to explore larger and larger even numbers, checking if they could consistently find pairs of primes that added up to these numbers. The more they searched, the more convinced they became that the conjecture might indeed be accurate.

As the story continues, mathematicians around the world are still on the quest to conclusively prove the Goldbach Conjecture for all even numbers. The mystery remains unsolved, but the journey continues, fueled by the excitement of unlocking the secrets hidden within the world of numbers and primes. And so, the mathematical adventure persists, with each calculation bringing them closer to uncovering the truth behind the Goldbach Conjecture.

$$\frac{x}{a} + \frac{y}{b} = 1$$

QUESTION 4

What was the true extent of the Library of Alexandria's collection, and what knowledge was lost when it was destroyed?

Once upon a time, there was a legendary library in the ancient city of Alexandria. This library was like a treasure trove of knowledge, filled with scrolls and books containing the collective wisdom of the ancient world. The people of Alexandria were proud of their library, which became a symbol of intellectual richness. The story begins with the library's founding by Ptolemy II in the 3rd century BCE. Scholars from all corners of the ancient world flocked to the Library of Alexandria, bringing with them texts on subjects ranging from philosophy and mathematics to astronomy and medicine. The library aimed to gather and preserve the entirety of human knowledge. As the library flourished, it housed an immense collection, becoming a beacon for scholars, philosophers, and researchers. The scrolls contained the works of famous thinkers like Euclid, Archimedes, and Eratosthenes, along with contributions from cultures around the Mediterranean and beyond. However, the story took a tragic turn during various moments in history, particularly during Julius Caesar's siege of Alexandria in 48 BCE. Legend has it that during the conflict, part of the library caught fire, leading to the destruction of a significant portion of its precious scrolls and manuscripts. While the exact details remain unclear, this event marked the beginning of the library's decline. The library faced further challenges with subsequent conflicts and political changes, and its once-vast collection gradually dwindled. The library that once stood as a symbol of intellectual achievement eventually faded away, leaving behind a legacy shrouded in mystery and loss.

What knowledge was lost in the destruction of the Library of Alexandria remains one of history's great mysteries. It's believed that countless works of ancient scholars, unique perspectives, and invaluable insights vanished with the library's decline. The destruction of the Library of Alexandria is a poignant reminder of how the loss of a single repository of knowledge can echo across centuries, leaving an indelible mark on the history of human understanding. And so, the story of the Library of Alexandria serves as a cautionary tale, urging us to cherish and protect the knowledge that enriches our collective human journey.

QUESTION 5

Can we achieve a complete understanding of the human brain and its functions?

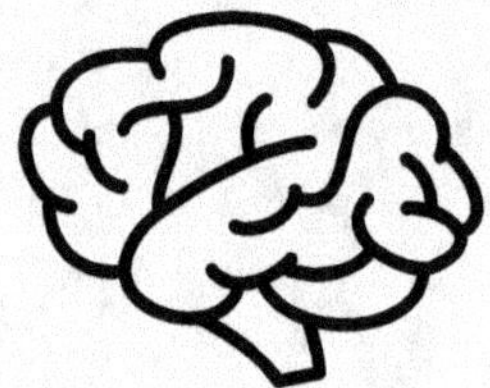

Once upon a time, scientists embarked on an exciting quest to unlock the mysteries of the human brain. Their journey began with exploring the brain's physical structure and evolved into understanding its intricate functions. Armed with tools like microscopes and imaging technologies, they delved into the complex network of billions of neurons.

As the adventure unfolded, scientists used various techniques like microscopes to study tiny neurons and imaging technologies like MRIs to capture the dance of neural circuits. Challenges arose as they deciphered the brain's intricate network of billions of neurons, each connecting to thousands of others.

Undeterred by challenges, scientists delved into genetics, studying the DNA instructions guiding the brain's development. They explored the delicate balance of chemicals influencing our moods and thoughts. Embracing interdisciplinary collaboration, neuroscientists joined forces with computer scientists, psychologists, and philosophers.

The brain, however, remains a puzzle with many missing pieces, leaving questions about consciousness, memory, and complex emotions. Despite this, scientists have made remarkable strides in unraveling the brain's intricacies. The adventure continues, promising new chapters in understanding the most remarkable organ in the universe. And so, the ongoing saga of understanding the human brain invites scientists and curious minds to explore the ever-deepening voyage into the heart of our consciousness.

QUESTION 6

What is the ultimate fate of the Riemann Hypothesis, one of the most famous and longstanding unsolved problems in mathematics?

In the enchanting world of mathematics, there lived a captivating mystery called the Riemann Hypothesis. This riddle focused on the distribution of prime numbers, those unique digits indivisible by any number except one and themselves. Bernhard Riemann, a brilliant mathematician from the 19th century, initiated the story by unveiling a hypothesis that could revolutionize the understanding of prime numbers. He proposed a specific pattern predicting where prime numbers like 2, 3, 5, and 7 would appear along an infinite number line. The mathematical community embarked on an intellectual adventure, realizing the Riemann Hypothesis was more than a puzzle – it was a gateway to unlocking the secrets of prime numbers and the fundamental nature of mathematics. This journey delved into the realm of complex numbers, where mathematicians explored the mysterious landscape of the Riemann zeta function. Despite intense scrutiny, no one could definitively prove or disprove the Riemann Hypothesis. It stood as one of the enduring unsolved problems in mathematics, tempting explorers with a million-dollar prize for cracking its enigmatic code. Mathematicians worldwide joined the quest, using computers and innovative techniques to scrutinize vast numerical data. Yet, the Riemann Hypothesis remained elusive, teasing mathematicians with its profound implications for number theory and cryptography.

Today, the story is one of anticipation and wonder. The Riemann Hypothesis continues to enthrall mathematicians, drawing them into a journey that transcends numbers and touches the essence of mathematical truth. Its ultimate fate remains uncertain, creating an enduring mystery that fuels exploration in the magical realm of mathematics. The tale persists, inviting mathematicians to unravel its secrets and uncover the deeper truths hidden within the numerical fabric of our universe.

$$m = \frac{f(x_2) - f(x_1)}{x_2 - x_1}$$

QUESTION 7

What is the nature of the mysterious "fast radio bursts" observed in distant galaxies?

Once upon a time, astronomers gazed into the vastness of space and stumbled upon a cosmic puzzle called "fast radio bursts" (FRBs). These were like celestial fireworks, brief bursts of powerful radio waves coming from distant galaxies, leaving scientists intrigued and mystified.

The story began in the early 2000s when astronomers first detected these energetic bursts, each lasting just a fraction of a second. The challenge was to uncover the source of these intense signals, as they released as much energy in milliseconds as the Sun does in an entire year.

To solve the cosmic mystery, scientists used powerful telescopes to spot more instances of fast radio bursts, revealing that they originated from galaxies far, far away. The question then became: What celestial phenomena could produce such energetic and rapid signals?

Various theories emerged. Some suggested highly magnetized neutron stars called magnetars, remnants of massive stars, might be behind the bursts. The intense magnetic fields around these exotic objects could generate the observed energetic signals.

Another idea floated the possibility of supermassive black holes at the centers of distant galaxies as the source. Extreme gravitational forces near these cosmic giants might be unleashing powerful energy in the form of radio waves.

The plot thickened when scientists discovered that some fast radio bursts repeated, emitting signals multiple times. This added complexity to the mystery, as the nature of these repeating bursts differed from the one-off events.

As the scientific adventure continued, researchers built advanced telescopes and collaborated globally to detect and study fast radio bursts. The quest led them to consider various cosmic scenarios, from colliding neutron stars to undiscovered celestial phenomena.

While progress has been made, the full story of fast radio bursts is still unfolding. The nature of these cosmic signals remains an exciting puzzle, drawing astronomers deeper into a cosmic tale filled with bursts of energy, distant galaxies, and the ongoing quest to understand the universe's secrets. And so, the saga of fast radio bursts continues, inviting scientists to delve into the cosmic expanse and reveal the celestial dramas behind these enigmatic signals.

QUESTION 8

Are all snowflakes different?

The mystery of whether all snowflakes are different is a captivating journey into the microscopic world of ice crystals. At the heart of this mystery lies the intricate process of snowflake formation, where tiny ice crystals begin their journey in the clouds. As these ice crystals fall through the atmosphere, they encounter varying temperature and humidity conditions, shaping their individual destinies.

The story unfolds in the molecular dance of water molecules, where the hexagonal symmetry of each molecule contributes to the mesmerizing patterns of snowflakes. While there are certain common patterns, the uniqueness arises from the specific atmospheric conditions each snowflake experiences during its descent. Imagine each snowflake as a tiny traveler, taking a one-of-a-kind journey through the sky, encountering different environments that sculpt its delicate structure.

While it's challenging to definitively prove that no two snowflakes are identical, the sheer number of possible variations and the ever-changing atmospheric conditions make it highly improbable. This mystery adds a touch of wonder to the winter landscape, reminding us of the incredible diversity hidden within the seemingly simple beauty of snowflakes, each telling a distinct tale of its atmospheric adventure.

QUESTION 9

Is there a unified theory that reconciles all fundamental forces in the universe?

Once upon a cosmic quest, scientists sought a grand unified theory to harmonize all fundamental forces in the universe. The story began with the recognition of distinct forces like gravity, electromagnetism, and nuclear forces, each playing a unique role. The challenge was to weave them together into a seamless framework. Albert Einstein's theory of general relativity explained gravity as the bending of spacetime, but it stood alone. Quantum mechanics handled electromagnetism at the microscopic level but kept gravity at bay, creating a cosmic gap.

String theory entered the stage, proposing a universe composed of vibrating strings at the tiniest scales. While promising unification, conclusive evidence remained elusive. The Standard Model successfully unified electromagnetism with weak and strong nuclear forces but left gravity unincorporated.

The cosmic journey continued with experiments and particle accelerators, aiming to reveal the secrets of the universe's fundamental forces. Despite progress, the grand unified theory remains a tantalizing dream. Gravity, the cosmic outlier, resists integration.

The ongoing story invites scientists worldwide to collaborate, unlocking the universe's fundamental secrets and bringing the cosmic tale to its grand conclusion. The quest for a unified theory endures, beckoning dreamers and scientists to join the cosmic adventure and reveal the ultimate blueprint governing our vast and mysterious universe.

QUESTION 10

Can we definitively identify the historical figure or figures behind the legend of King Arthur, separating fact from myth?

Once upon a time, in the pages of history and legend, there was a captivating tale of King Arthur, a legendary figure surrounded by myths and mysteries. The story unfolded in a quest to uncover the truth behind this iconic character and separate the factual threads from the fabric of myth. The historical journey began in medieval times, where stories of King Arthur and his knights became woven into the cultural tapestry of Britain. However, as historians delved into ancient manuscripts and chronicles, they encountered a challenge – the line between historical fact and mythical embellishment became blurred.

One contender for the historical Arthur was a warrior-leader from the late 5th to early 6th centuries, a tumultuous period in Britain's history. This Arthur was seen as a hero who fought against invading forces, and some historical sources vaguely hinted at his existence. However, the evidence was sparse, leaving room for skepticism and debate. The story took an intriguing turn with the discovery of archaeological sites and artifacts, hinting at a complex society in post-Roman Britain. Some historians suggested that elements of the Arthurian legends might have been inspired by real events and figures from this tumultuous time.

As the tale continued, scholars explored ancient texts, such as Geoffrey of Monmouth's "Historia Regum Britanniae" and the Welsh "Annales Cambriae," seeking clues about the historical Arthur. These texts, while laden with fantastical elements, added layers to the mystery, prompting historians to decipher the historical nuggets within the mythical narrative. Yet, the elusive nature of King Arthur persisted. The lack of concrete evidence and the blending of history with folklore created a landscape where the line between reality and legend remained shrouded. In the end, the quest to definitively identify the historical figure or figures behind the legend of King Arthur remains an ongoing challenge. The story stands as a testament to the enduring power of myth and the complexities of untangling historical truths from the tapestry of storytelling. The legend of King Arthur lives on, inviting historians and dreamers alike to explore the mysterious realms where history and myth intertwine.

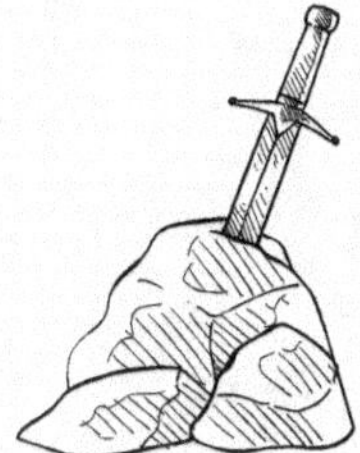

QUESTION 11

What is the true nature of mathematical infinity, and how do different sizes of infinity compare and interact with each other?

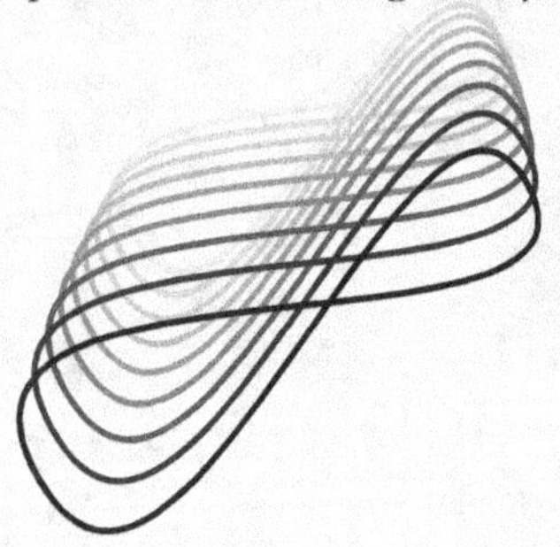

Once upon a time in the vast world of mathematics, there was a captivating concept called infinity. It wasn't just a really big number; it represented an endless, boundless quantity, transcending any numerical boundary.

The story unfolded with Georg Cantor, a visionary mathematician who introduced the idea that not all infinities are the same size. He ingeniously compared infinities by pairing up their elements, revealing a hierarchy of sizes within the infinite realm. For instance, he showed that the infinity of real numbers between 0 and 1 is larger than the infinity of natural numbers (1, 2, 3, ...).

The tale took an enchanting turn when Cantor introduced the concept of "uncountable" infinities, demonstrating that not all infinities can be matched up in a straightforward way. This revelation expanded our understanding of the diverse sizes within the infinite realm.

Cantor's work sparked a profound dialogue among mathematicians, leading to the exploration of mathematical landscapes where infinities interacted and intertwined. Set theory, a framework introduced by Cantor, became a powerful tool to navigate the intricate relationships between different sizes of infinity.

As the mathematical adventure continues, infinity remains a tantalizing concept, offering both simplicity and profound complexity. The idea that there are various sizes of infinity challenges our intuition and opens up new avenues for understanding the boundless nature of mathematics. And so, the story of mathematical infinity unfolds, with mathematicians embarking on an endless exploration, uncovering the mysteries that lie beyond the realm of finite numbers.

QUESTION 12

What is the true nature of the so-called "Planet Nine" hypothesized to exist in the outer solar system?

Once upon a time in our solar system, astronomers stumbled upon a cosmic mystery – the intriguing tale of "Planet Nine." The story began with observations of outer planets and distant objects, revealing unusual patterns in their orbits. Something seemed to be affecting their movements beyond the known planets. Astronomers, armed with curiosity, hypothesized the existence of an unseen ninth planet, named Planet Nine. This hypothetical world, much larger than Earth, was believed to lurk in the outer solar system, far beyond Neptune's orbit.

The plot thickened as scientists delved into data, examining the orbits of distant icy bodies like Kuiper Belt objects. Peculiarities in their paths hinted at the gravitational influence of an unseen giant – Planet Nine.

The hunt for Planet Nine turned into a cosmic quest, with astronomers using telescopes and simulations to pinpoint its potential location and characteristics.

However, despite extensive efforts, the true nature of Planet Nine remained hidden. The story continued with tantalizing hints and indirect evidence, but as of now, no direct observation or conclusive proof of Planet Nine has been found.

The tale of Planet Nine is one of cosmic intrigue and ongoing exploration. Astronomers persist in peering into the outer solar system, eager to unveil the secrets of this elusive celestial neighbor. And so, the story of Planet Nine beckons scientists and sky watchers to join the quest for understanding the mysteries that reside beyond the familiar bounds of our solar system.

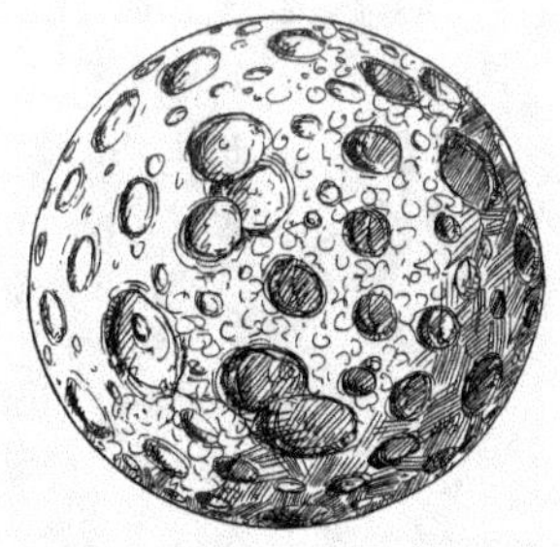

QUESTION 13

How do certain animals, like octopuses, exhibit highly intelligent and adaptive behaviors despite having a very different neural structure than mammals?

Once upon a time in the ocean's depths, a tale unfolded about creatures like the octopus – intelligent beings with a neural structure unlike mammals. Scientists embarked on a journey to understand how these animals exhibited remarkable intelligence and adaptability.

The adventure began with the realization that octopuses have a decentralized nervous system. Unlike mammals, their neurons are spread throughout their bodies, offering a unique way of processing information.

As the scientific expedition continued, researchers marveled at the problem-solving abilities of octopuses. Despite their different neural structure, these clever creatures could escape enclosures, blend seamlessly with their surroundings, and manipulate objects with their flexible arms.

The story took an intriguing turn as scientists studied the complexity of octopus brains. Despite lacking the intricate folds of mammalian brains, octopuses possessed highly evolved brains with a large number of neurons, enabling sophisticated information processing.

Scientists also discovered the octopus's remarkable capacity to learn through observation and experience. These creatures adapted their behaviors based on their surroundings, solving puzzles, and even opening jars to access hidden treats, showcasing their learning and memory abilities.

The tale deepened as researchers explored the idea that octopuses might have a form of consciousness. Their behaviors hinted at a level of awareness and decision-making that challenged traditional views of animal intelligence.

In the end, the story of intelligent octopuses became a narrative of adaptation and ingenuity. Despite their distinct neural structure, these creatures exhibited remarkable problem-solving skills, learning abilities, and adaptive behaviors that defied expectations. The mystery of how octopuses manifest their intelligence continues to captivate scientists, inviting them to dive deeper into the ocean's depths and unlock the secrets of these extraordinary beings. And so, the saga of intelligent octopuses persists, a testament to the diverse and awe-inspiring intelligence that exists in the animal kingdom.

QUESTION 14

Are there dimensions beyond the ones we perceive?

Once upon a time in the universe, a profound mystery unfolded – the exploration of dimensions beyond our perception. Scientists ventured into the fabric of reality, questioning whether there could be more to the world than our three-dimensional experience. The adventure began with the acknowledgment of our familiar three-dimensional world, where objects have length, width, and height. But physicists, fueled by curiosity, pondered the existence of hidden dimensions beyond our everyday senses. The story took an intriguing turn with the introduction of string theory. This theoretical framework proposed that the universe's fundamental building blocks are not point-like particles but tiny, vibrating strings. String theory suggested the presence of extra dimensions, beyond the three we know, intricately woven and not directly observable.

Imagine these extra dimensions as concealed realms, compact and curled up, influencing the forces and particles we observe in our observable universe. Although these dimensions are beyond direct perception, their effects might manifest in the behavior of the fundamental forces.

Scientists envisioned these hidden dimensions as tiny, coiled structures that could potentially solve some cosmic mysteries, such as the nature of gravity and the unification of fundamental forces.

The tale continued with the pursuit of experimental evidence. Physicists sought clues in high-energy particle collisions and the behavior of fundamental particles, hoping to catch a glimpse of these elusive dimensions. As of now, direct evidence remains elusive, and the extra dimensions stay concealed, holding their secrets. The story of dimensions beyond perception invites contemplation about the nature of reality. While our everyday experiences are confined to three dimensions, the possibility of hidden realms adds a layer of mystery to the universe's fabric. The quest to understand these concealed dimensions persists, an exploration into the unseen corners of reality that may one day unveil cosmic secrets hidden in dimensions beyond our perception.

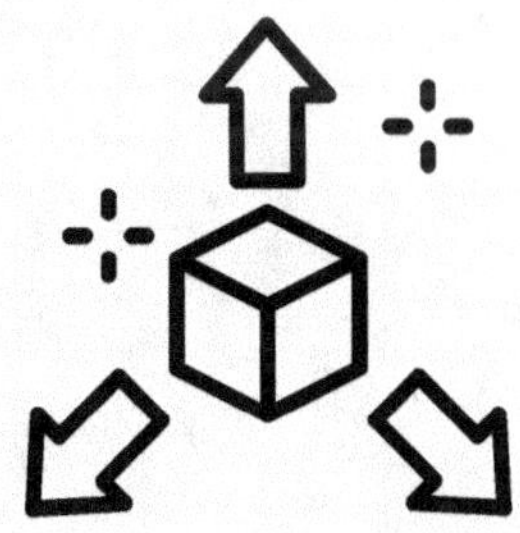

QUESTION 15

What was the purpose and content of the ancient Voynich Manuscript, and can its mysterious script be deciphered?

Once upon a time, a mysterious book named the Voynich Manuscript emerged, filled with intricate illustrations of plants, celestial bodies, and enigmatic human-like figures. Scholars and code-breakers embarked on a quest to unravel its purpose and content, encountering a script that resisted decipherment.

Discovered in the early 20th century, the Voynich Manuscript baffled researchers with its unfamiliar script, resembling no known language. Despite numerous attempts, the characters remained a cryptic puzzle, giving rise to theories ranging from an ancient herbal guide to an elaborate hoax.

Carbon dating placed the manuscript's origin in the 15th century, deepening the mystery. Scholars explored its pages, attempting to extract valuable knowledge or discern its purpose. However, the enigmatic script continued to guard its secrets.

Technological advancements brought new tools, allowing scholars to study the manuscript in greater detail. Despite advanced imaging and digital analysis revealing more about its physical characteristics, the linguistic and thematic mysteries endured.

In the current cosmic chapter, the purpose and content of the Voynich Manuscript remain elusive. The undeciphered script continues to intrigue and inspire, embodying a narrative of historical puzzles and scholarly quests. The manuscript's mysterious pages beckon curious minds to join the ongoing exploration of this ancient riddle. And so, the manuscript's secrets persist, whispering cryptic tales across the ages.

QUESTION 16

What is the meaning of consciousness?

Once upon a time, a profound question echoed through human inquiry – the meaning of consciousness. This story unfolds as philosophers, scientists, and thinkers embarked on a quest to fathom the essence of consciousness, the mysterious awareness that defines our existence.

The adventure began with the recognition that consciousness is more than mere wakefulness. It involves the ability to experience, perceive, and have subjective thoughts and feelings. The question emerged: What gives rise to this inner world of thoughts and sensations?

As the narrative unfolded, philosophers like Descartes pondered the inseparable link between thought and existence. Others, like Locke and Hume, explored how experiences shape consciousness, laying the groundwork for the idea that the mind is a product of sensory input.

The story took an intriguing turn with the rise of neuroscience. Scientists delved into the brain, searching for the neural mechanisms behind consciousness. They found that consciousness is intricately linked to the brain's activity, with different regions contributing to various aspects of our awareness.

Yet, the mystery deepened with the "hard problem" of consciousness – the inquiry into why and how brain processes give rise to subjective experience. Thinkers like David Chalmers proposed that consciousness might be a fundamental aspect of the universe, beyond physical explanations.

As the quest continued, artificial intelligence entered the stage, probing whether machines could possess a form of consciousness. The story grappled with ethical questions about the nature of consciousness and the implications of creating self-aware entities.

In the present cosmic chapter, the meaning of consciousness remains an open question. It is a tale of exploration, weaving together philosophy, neuroscience, and ethics. The quest for understanding consciousness invites us to ponder the essence of our own awareness and the mysteries within our minds. And so, the story of consciousness continues, a journey into the heart of what it means to be truly alive and aware in the vast tapestry of existence.

QUESTION 17

What caused the mysterious collapse of the ancient Indus Valley Civilization, and what was the nature of its written language?

Once upon a time, in the ancient land of the Indus Valley, a flourishing civilization emerged, marked by advanced cities, sophisticated architecture, and a mysterious script. This story unfolds as historians and archaeologists embark on a quest to unravel the causes behind the enigmatic collapse of the Indus Valley Civilization and decode the nature of its written language.

The adventure began with the discovery of the ancient ruins in what is now Pakistan and northwest India. Archaeologists uncovered evidence of well-planned cities, advanced sewage systems, and intricate trade networks, suggesting a thriving civilization dating back to around 3300 BCE.

As the narrative unfolded, clues about the collapse of the Indus Valley Civilization surfaced. The once-bustling cities, like Mohenjo-Daro and Harappa, showed signs of decline around 1900 BCE. The reasons behind this decline are still debated, with theories ranging from environmental changes and ecological factors to possible invasions or social upheavals.

The story took an intriguing turn with the decipherment attempts of the Indus script. The civilization's written language, etched onto seals and artifacts, remained a mystery for a long time. Unlike other ancient scripts, scholars have struggled to decode the Indus script, as its symbols do not align with known languages of the time.

Despite efforts, the nature of the Indus script remains elusive, adding an extra layer of mystery to the tale. The symbols have not been definitively linked to any known language, leaving the content and meaning of the inscriptions largely unknown.

As the current chapter stands, the collapse of the Indus Valley Civilization and the enigma of its written language persist. The story is one of archaeological puzzles and linguistic mysteries, inviting curious minds to delve into the ancient remnants and unlock the secrets of a civilization that once thrived along the banks of the mighty Indus River. And so, the saga of the Indus Valley Civilization continues, a tapestry woven with both the brilliance of its achievements and the mysteries that time has yet to fully reveal.

QUESTION 18

How does quantum entanglement work on a macroscopic scale?

Once upon a time in the captivating realm of quantum physics, there existed a fascinating phenomenon called quantum entanglement. This story unfolds as scientists delve into the mysterious world of entanglement, aiming to understand how it operates on a larger, more visible scale.

The adventure begins with the fundamental concept of quantum entanglement – a unique connection between particles where the state of one instantaneously influences the state of another, regardless of the distance between them. Initially observed in tiny particles like electrons and photons, entanglement posed questions about its potential extension to larger, more macroscopic objects.

As the narrative progresses, scientists explore the possibility of entanglement beyond the microscopic world. This challenges classical intuitions, suggesting that the interconnected behavior observed in the quantum realm could manifest in larger, more tangible objects visible to the naked eye.

The story takes an intriguing turn as experiments test the boundaries of entanglement. Researchers work to entangle larger particles or groups of particles, pushing the limits of our understanding. Cooling larger particles to ultra-cold temperatures is one approach, bringing them into a quantum state where entanglement becomes more pronounced.

However, the tale encounters challenges. Maintaining and observing entanglement on a macroscopic scale proves delicate, requiring precise control over experimental conditions. The inherent uncertainties of the quantum world introduce complexities that continue to puzzle scientists.

In the current chapter, the story of quantum entanglement on a macroscopic scale remains a topic of ongoing exploration and debate. The quest continues to comprehend how the peculiar principles of quantum physics might influence objects visible to our eyes. The story of macroscopic quantum entanglement is a journey into the mysterious and counterintuitive nature of the quantum world, inviting us to reconsider our understanding of reality. And so, the saga of quantum entanglement expands, with each experiment and discovery adding new chapters to the captivating tale of the quantum realm.

QUESTION 19

What is the true nature of time?

Once upon a time, in the vast expanse of the universe, a profound mystery beckoned – the true nature of time. This story unfolds as scientists, philosophers, and thinkers embark on a quest to unravel the essence of time, that ever-flowing river shaping our experiences. The adventure begins with the simple observation that time appears to move forward, from past through present to future. However, deeper questions emerge. What is time beyond our human perception? Does it exist independently, ticking away like a cosmic clock? The narrative takes an intriguing turn with Einstein's theory of relativity. He proposes that time is intertwined with space, creating a fabric known as spacetime. Here, gravity warps both space and time, influencing how clocks tick in different gravitational conditions. As the quest unfolds, the nature of time becomes more elusive. Quantum mechanics, exploring the microscopic world, presents a different perspective where past, present, and future coexist. The notion of a "block universe" challenges our intuitive sense of linear progression. The tale encounters the arrow of time – the asymmetry between past and future. Scientists grapple with the puzzle of why time seemingly moves in one direction, from order to disorder, as dictated by the second law of thermodynamics.

Yet, the story is not without paradoxes. Time, it seems, is entangled with the fabric of reality in ways that defy straightforward explanations. Philosophers ponder whether time is an emergent property or a fundamental aspect of the cosmos.

As the cosmic chapters unfold, the true nature of time remains a captivating mystery. It is a tale of exploration intertwining with the fabric of the universe, inviting us to ponder the essence of this elusive force governing our existence. The story of time is a journey into the heart of our temporal reality, where past, present, and future dance together in the cosmic ballet of existence. And so, the saga of time continues, a timeless narrative that transcends the ticking of clocks and beckons us to explore the depths of the temporal enigma.

QUESTION 20

Can every polynomial equation with integer coefficients have at least one solution in integers, as proposed by the generalized Ramanujan–Nagell equation?

Once upon a mathematical journey, a captivating question emerged: Can every polynomial equation with integer coefficients possess at least one solution in integers? The narrative unfolds with the exploration of this puzzle, and mathematicians find inspiration in the generalized Ramanujan–Nagell equation. In this mathematical adventure, polynomial equations took center stage, posing the intriguing inquiry of whether solutions in integers could always be found. Enter the generalized Ramanujan–Nagell equation, a tool guiding mathematicians in understanding the characteristics of integer solutions for specific types of polynomials.

As the story progresses, mathematicians dive into the complexities of these equations, using the generalized Ramanujan–Nagell equation as a beacon. While it provides insights into certain scenarios, proving the general case for all polynomial equations remains an intricate challenge.

Armed with the tools of number theory and algebra, researchers scrutinize the relationships between coefficients and solutions, searching for patterns that could unravel the mystery of when integer solutions are universally possible.

In the current mathematical chapter, the question persists, and mathematicians continue their quest to unveil the truth. The generalized Ramanujan–Nagell equation stands as a guide, sparking curiosity and inspiring mathematicians to unravel the secrets of integer solutions in the captivating world of polynomials. The saga of this mathematical inquiry continues to evolve, with each theorem and proof contributing to the unfolding story of polynomial equations and their integer solutions. And so, the mathematical journey persists, inviting minds to join the exploration of equations in the realm of integers.

QUESTION 21

Is there a fundamental connection between the macroscopic world governed by classical physics and the microscopic realm of quantum mechanics?

In the vast realm of physics, a captivating question arises: Is there a fundamental link between the familiar world governed by classical physics and the mysterious microscopic domain of quantum mechanics? Physicists embark on a journey, starting with the predictable principles of classical physics that describe everyday objects with well-defined properties. As the narrative unfolds, they delve into the intricacies of quantum mechanics, where particles exhibit behaviors like superposition and uncertainty, challenging our classical intuition. The quest centers on understanding the transition between these two realms, exploring concepts such as decoherence as a potential bridge. Despite the challenges posed by fundamentally different principles, scientists persist in their exploration, offering a fascinating tale of discovery and curiosity.

In the ongoing scientific saga, the question persists: How does the macroscopic world seamlessly emerge from the quantum realm? This journey into the heart of nature's mysteries invites curious minds to join the quest for a unified understanding of the physical world. As physicists navigate the quantum-to-classical transition, each discovery adds new chapters to the captivating narrative, bringing us closer to unraveling the connection between classical physics and the enigmatic world of quantum mechanics.

QUESTION 22

What caused the mysterious disappearance of Malaysian Airlines Flight MH370, and where is the wreckage located?

The disappearance of Malaysian Airlines Flight MH370 is still a mystery, and the exact cause is unknown. However, here's a simplified explanation of the events:

On March 8, 2014, MH370 took off from Kuala Lumpur, Malaysia, heading to Beijing, China. About an hour into the flight, the plane lost contact with air traffic control and disappeared from radar screens.

Investigators believe that someone deliberately turned off the plane's communication systems. The plane then made a series of unusual turns and flew for several hours, eventually running out of fuel and crashing into the southern Indian Ocean.

Despite extensive search efforts, the wreckage was not found for a long time. In July 2015, a piece of the plane's wing, called a flaperon, washed ashore on Reunion Island in the Indian Ocean. More debris, including other wing parts and a few confirmed pieces of the plane, has since been found along the coasts of Africa and islands in the Indian Ocean.

The main wreckage, however, has not been located, and the exact reasons behind the plane's disappearance remain unclear. The disappearance of MH370 has led to ongoing discussions and efforts to improve aircraft tracking systems and international coordination to prevent similar incidents in the future.

QUESTION 23

Is there a definitive answer to the age-old philosophical question: Why does anything exist at all rather than nothing?

The age-old philosophical question of why anything exists at all rather than nothing has intrigued thinkers for centuries. Different perspectives have been offered by religious, philosophical, and scientific traditions, each attempting to grapple with the mystery of existence.

From a religious standpoint, various beliefs posit that the existence of everything is tied to the will or purpose of a higher power or deity. In these frameworks, the universe and everything within it are seen as intentional creations with a specific divine purpose.

Philosophers, on the other hand, have delved into the nature of "nothing" itself, questioning whether the concept of absolute nothingness is coherent. Some wonder whether there has always been something, challenging the very idea of a state devoid of existence.

In the realm of scientific inquiry, cosmology provides insights into the origin and structure of the universe. The widely accepted Big Bang theory describes the universe's expansion from an extremely hot and dense state. However, this theory doesn't address why the initial conditions for the Big Bang existed, leaving the question of ultimate causation unanswered.

Quantum physics introduces a different perspective by revealing the complex and dynamic nature of the seemingly empty space. According to certain theories, even a vacuum is not truly empty but contains fluctuations and virtual particles, challenging traditional notions of nothingness.

Some theoretical physicists propose the concept of a multiverse, where our universe is just one of countless others. In a multiverse scenario, the question of why anything exists might be reframed as why our particular universe exists among myriad possible alternatives.

Despite these explorations, a definitive answer remains elusive. The quest to understand why anything exists continues to be a subject of deep contemplation, sparking ongoing discussions and investigations in philosophy, theology, and science. As our understanding of the universe evolves, new perspectives may emerge, but the fundamental mystery of existence endures.

QUESTION 24

How do certain plants and fungi possess medicinal properties, and can we fully understand the intricacies of their biochemical interactions with the human body?

Plants and fungi often have medicinal properties because they produce chemicals that help them survive and can also benefit the human body. Traditional healers noticed these effects over time, leading to the use of plants as medicines in different cultures. In modern science, researchers study these medicinal properties more systematically. They use advanced tools to identify and analyze specific compounds in plants and fungi that contribute to their therapeutic effects. For example, aspirin, a pain-reliever, was derived from a compound found in willow bark, and penicillin, an antibiotic, comes from a fungus called Penicillium.

The study of these interactions involves chemistry, pharmacology, and biochemistry. Scientists isolate and identify active compounds, study their effects on the human body, and explore potential medical uses.

However, fully understanding these interactions is an ongoing process. The human body is complex, and how plant and fungal compounds interact with it is not fully understood. Researchers continue working to identify beneficial compounds, understand how they work, and explore potential side effects.

QUESTION 25

What is the origin and nature of the mysterious signals known as cosmic rays, and how do they impact the cosmos?

Cosmic rays are mysterious signals that come from space, and they're made up of tiny particles like protons and atomic nuclei. These particles travel at incredibly high speeds, close to the speed of light. Scientists have been curious about where these cosmic rays come from and how they affect the cosmos. The story of understanding cosmic rays began a long time ago when scientists noticed unusual radiation coming from space. In the early 20th century, they started to figure out that these rays were actually charged particles zooming through space.

To study cosmic rays, scientists use detectors on Earth and even send instruments into space. They've discovered that cosmic rays can come from various sources, like exploding stars called supernovae or even distant galaxies. When these cosmic events happen, they release powerful energy, and some of it takes the form of these speedy particles we call cosmic rays.

Now, when these cosmic rays reach our atmosphere, they can interact with air molecules and create a cascade of other particles. This is what scientists detect with their instruments on Earth. It's like a cosmic dance happening above us, and by studying this dance, scientists can learn more about the distant and energetic events in the universe.

Cosmic rays impact the cosmos in a few ways. First, they give us valuable information about the most energetic processes occurring in space, helping scientists piece together the bigger picture of our universe. Second, cosmic rays can influence our space environment and even affect technology like satellites.

In summary, cosmic rays are speedy particles coming from various cosmic events, and by studying them, scientists gain insights into the energetic processes shaping our universe. It's like catching a glimpse of the cosmic ballet that happens far beyond our planet.

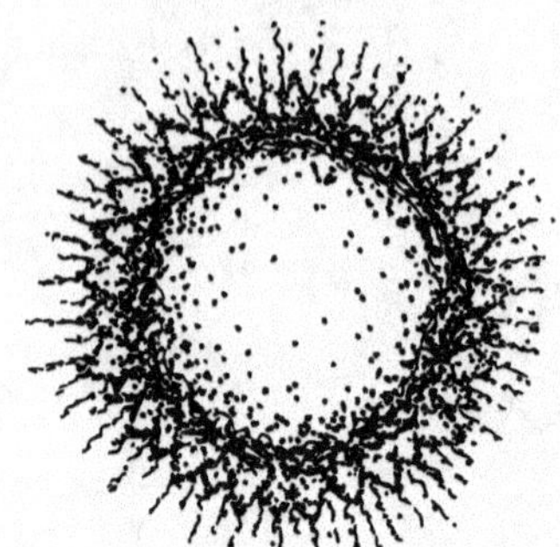

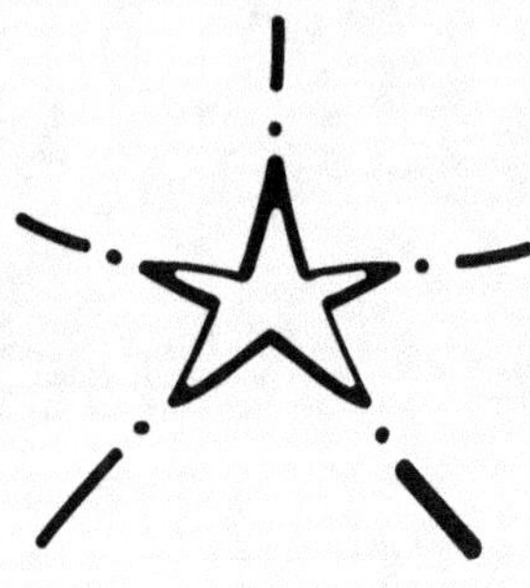

QUESTION 26

Can we definitively identify the historical figure behind the legend of William Tell, separating historical facts from folklore?

The legend of William Tell is a famous story that has been passed down through generations, blending history and folklore. While there is a historical background, separating fact from fiction can be challenging.

William Tell is said to be a skilled archer from Switzerland who defied a tyrannical ruler named Gessler. According to the legend, Gessler placed a hat on a pole and demanded that all passersby bow to it. When William Tell refused, he was ordered to shoot an apple off his son's head with his bow and arrow, showcasing his exceptional marksmanship.

Now, when it comes to identifying the historical figure behind this legend, it's not so straightforward. The story of William Tell emerged during the medieval period, and historical records from that time are limited and sometimes mixed with mythical elements.

There's debate among historians about whether William Tell was a real person or if the legend is a combination of various stories and characters. Some believe that there might have been an archer who resisted a tyrant, but the details are uncertain. The challenge in separating fact from folklore lies in the lack of concrete historical evidence. While Switzerland does have a history of standing up against oppressive rulers, the specific events of William Tell's tale are not well-documented.

In essence, the legend of William Tell has become a symbol of resistance and the fight for freedom, even if the precise details of the historical figure behind the story remain elusive. It's a reminder of the power of storytelling to capture the spirit of a people and their struggle for liberty.

QUESTION 27

What is the true nature of the enigmatic phenomenon known as dark energy, driving the accelerated expansion of the universe?

Dark energy is a mysterious force that scientists believe is causing the universe to expand at an accelerating rate. Understanding the true nature of dark energy is a complex puzzle that researchers have been trying to solve.

The story of dark energy begins with the observation that the universe is expanding. Scientists expected that the expansion might slow down over time due to gravity, but in the late 1990s, observations of distant exploding stars called supernovae revealed something unexpected: the expansion was speeding up.

To explain this acceleration, scientists proposed the existence of dark energy. Dark energy is thought to be a kind of energy that fills space and pushes galaxies away from each other, causing the accelerated expansion.

However, the true nature of dark energy remains elusive. It's called "dark" because it doesn't interact with light or other forms of electromagnetic radiation that scientists can easily detect. This makes it challenging to study directly.

One idea is that dark energy could be related to the vacuum of space itself, possessing a constant energy density. Another possibility is a property known as the cosmological constant, first introduced by Albert Einstein in his equations of general relativity. The cosmological constant represents a constant energy density that might be driving the acceleration.

Scientists use powerful telescopes and observatories to gather data on the large-scale structure of the universe, the distribution of galaxies, and the cosmic microwave background radiation to learn more about dark energy. These observations help refine our understanding of the expansion and the role dark energy plays.

In simple terms, dark energy is like an unseen force pushing galaxies apart and causing the universe to expand faster. While scientists have made significant progress, the full story of dark energy is still unfolding, and its true nature remains one of the biggest mysteries in cosmology.

QUESTION 28

Can we uncover the ancient technology used to construct monumental structures like the pyramids of Egypt, and what knowledge might it reveal about our past?

The construction of monumental structures like the pyramids of Egypt is a fascinating mystery, and while many aspects of the ancient technology used remain unknown, researchers have made some discoveries. The story of uncovering ancient construction methods involves a mix of archaeological findings and scientific investigations. The Egyptian pyramids, including the famous ones at Giza, were built thousands of years ago using massive stones, some weighing several tons. Understanding how ancient people transported and lifted these heavy stones has been a subject of much exploration. Researchers have found evidence that sledges and wooden sleds were likely used to transport the large stones across the desert. They believe workers wet the sand in front of the sledges to reduce friction, making it easier to move the heavy loads. This method has been demonstrated in experiments, showing that it's a plausible way to move large stones with fewer people. When it comes to lifting the stones to build the pyramids, scholars think ramps might have been used. These ramps could have been straight or zigzagging structures built alongside the pyramid, allowing workers to move the stones upward gradually. However, the exact design of these ramps is still a matter of debate among archaeologists. As for the precision in construction, the ancient Egyptians displayed remarkable mathematical and engineering skills. The alignment of the pyramids with the cardinal points (north, south, east, west) and the precision in stone cutting and placement are evidence of advanced knowledge.

Uncovering the ancient technology used to build these structures provides valuable insights into the capabilities of past civilizations. It showcases their ingenuity, organizational abilities, and understanding of engineering principles. While some details remain unclear, ongoing research continues to shed light on the methods employed by ancient people to create these enduring monuments, contributing to our understanding of human history and technological development.

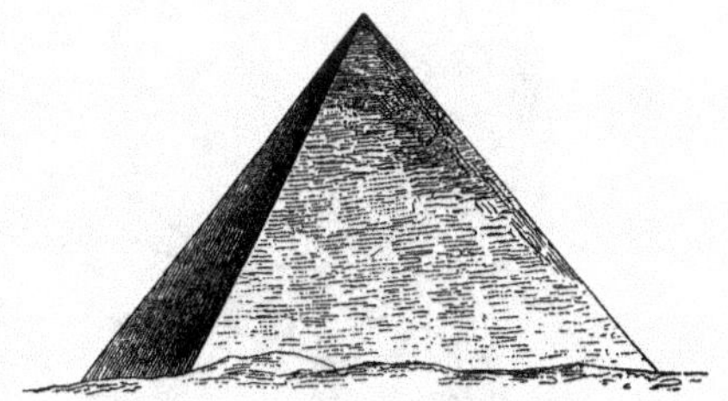

QUESTION 29

How do some animals, like monarch butterflies, navigate vast distances during migration using complex navigation mechanisms, and can we fully understand these processes?

Monarch butterflies are amazing creatures that travel incredibly long distances during their migration. Understanding how they navigate such vast distances involves a mix of observation and scientific investigation.

The story of monarch butterfly navigation starts with their ability to use the sun as a compass. During the day, they can sense the position of the sun in the sky, helping them determine direction. This is like having a built-in sun compass that guides them on their journey. But what about when the sun isn't visible, like on cloudy days or during the night? Monarchs also use other strategies. One is based on the Earth's magnetic field — they seem to have a magnetic compass that helps them stay on course. Scientists believe they can sense the Earth's magnetic field and use it as an additional navigation tool. Interestingly, monarch butterflies also seem to be able to recognize landmarks and use them for orientation. This might include mountains, rivers, or even human-made structures. By remembering and recognizing these features, they can adjust their route accordingly.

The story of understanding these navigation processes involves researchers using various tools. They've done experiments where they manipulate the position of the sun or create artificial magnetic fields to see how it affects the butterflies' ability to navigate. They also study the behavior of butterflies in controlled environments to learn more about their preferences and capabilities.

While we've made significant progress in understanding monarch butterfly navigation, the complete picture is still unfolding. These tiny creatures possess complex mechanisms that help them embark on incredible journeys. The ongoing research not only teaches us about the amazing abilities of butterflies but also provides insights into broader questions about animal navigation and migration. It's like uncovering the secrets of a small, winged explorer and learning more about the wonders of the natural world.

QUESTION 30

What is the origin of the mysterious, unexplained phenomenon known as ball lightning, and how does it manifest in the natural world?

Ball lightning is a strange and unexplained phenomenon that has puzzled scientists for a long time. The story of understanding ball lightning involves reports from people who claim to have seen glowing balls of light, often spherical in shape, during thunderstorms or sometimes indoors. Researchers have been trying to figure out what causes ball lightning and how it manifests in the natural world. The challenge is that ball lightning is rare and unpredictable, making it difficult to study. However, there are a few theories based on observations and limited experiments. One theory suggests that during thunderstorms, electrical charges in the air may create plasma—a super-hot, ionized gas. This plasma could form a glowing ball that floats in the air for a short time. Another idea is that certain chemical reactions in the atmosphere might produce these luminous orbs.

Some reports describe ball lightning appearing inside homes, not just during storms. In these cases, researchers wonder if certain conditions, like electrical discharges or the presence of certain gases, could lead to the formation of these mysterious balls of light. The challenge in understanding ball lightning lies in its elusive and unpredictable nature. Scientists are working on recreating the conditions that might lead to its formation in controlled experiments, but it's a complex puzzle that hasn't been fully solved yet.

In simple terms, ball lightning is like a glowing ball that appears mysteriously, often during thunderstorms or even indoors. Scientists are trying to uncover the secrets behind this phenomenon by studying reports, conducting experiments, and exploring the conditions that might lead to the creation of these luminous spheres in the natural world. It's a captivating mystery that continues to intrigue researchers and those fascinated by the wonders of nature.

QUESTION 31

What is the precise mechanism behind the placebo effect, and how can the mind influence physical health and healing?

The placebo effect is a fascinating phenomenon where a person experiences improvements in their condition after receiving a treatment that has no active ingredients. The story of understanding the placebo effect involves exploring how the mind can influence physical health and healing. When a person believes that a treatment is effective, their brain can trigger real physiological changes in the body. For example, if someone thinks they are taking a pain-relieving pill, their brain might release natural chemicals, like endorphins, which can help reduce pain. Scientists have conducted studies to unravel the mechanisms behind the placebo effect. One key aspect is the brain's ability to produce neurotransmitters and other chemicals that impact the body's functions. Believing in the effectiveness of a treatment can activate these natural healing processes.

The brain and body are closely connected through a network of signals. When the brain perceives that a treatment is beneficial, it sends signals to various systems in the body, influencing things like pain perception, inflammation, and even immune responses. In simple terms, the mind can play a powerful role in promoting healing. The placebo effect shows that our beliefs and expectations can influence how our bodies respond to treatments. Understanding this connection between the mind and physical health has led to a growing appreciation for the role of psychological factors in medical care.

Researchers are continuing to explore the placebo effect to better understand its mechanisms and potential applications in healthcare. While it doesn't replace the need for effective medical treatments, recognizing the mind's impact on healing opens up new possibilities for optimizing patient care and well-being. It's like discovering the mind's hidden ability to contribute to the body's natural healing processes.

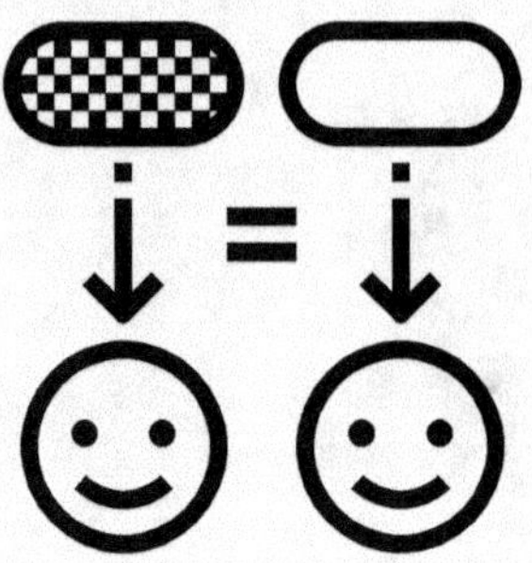

QUESTION 32

Can we unlock the secrets of dreams, understanding their purpose, the nature of consciousness during sleep, and the role they play in our mental and emotional well-being?

Unlocking the secrets of dreams has been a curious journey for scientists and researchers. The story involves exploring the purpose of dreams, understanding the nature of consciousness during sleep, and recognizing the role dreams play in our mental and emotional well-being.

Dreams happen during a phase of sleep called REM (Rapid Eye Movement) sleep. Scientists believe that during this time, our brains are very active, even though our bodies are still and relaxed. This is when most vivid and memorable dreams occur.

One idea about the purpose of dreams is that they might help with memory consolidation and learning. Dreams could be a way for our brains to process and organize information from the day, kind of like a mental clean-up. They might also be a way for us to practice and prepare for challenges we might face.

Understanding the nature of consciousness during sleep involves studying brain activity. While we're asleep, our brains go through different stages, and during REM sleep, the brain is buzzing with activity, almost like when we're awake. However, our consciousness is altered, and our ability to control our thoughts is reduced. Dreams can be vivid, emotional experiences, and they often tap into our fears, hopes, and daily experiences. They can be like a movie playing in our minds.

Researchers use brain imaging and monitoring tools to study these dream processes, trying to uncover the connections between brain activity and the content of our dreams.

In terms of mental and emotional well-being, dreams can provide insights into our thoughts and emotions. They might serve as a kind of emotional release, helping us process feelings or concerns. Nightmares, for example, could be a way for the brain to deal with stress or fears.

While the full story of dreams is still unfolding, researchers are making progress in understanding their purpose and role in our lives. Studying dreams involves a mix of psychology, neuroscience, and sleep research, and it's like deciphering a code that our minds create every night. The secrets of dreams continue to capture the fascination of scientists and offer glimpses into the mysteries of our consciousness during sleep.

QUESTION 33

Is there a limit to human longevity, and can we extend the human lifespan significantly through scientific advancements?

The question of human longevity—how long people can live—is a topic that scientists have explored for a long time. The story involves understanding the factors that influence aging and whether we can significantly extend human lifespan through scientific advancements. Firstly, it's important to know that the maximum human lifespan observed so far is around 120 years. This doesn't mean everyone can live that long, but it's the oldest age recorded. The factors influencing aging are complex and include genetic, environmental, and lifestyle components.

Scientists have been studying the biology of aging to figure out how and why our bodies age. Some believe that aging is a result of the gradual accumulation of damage to our cells and tissues over time. This damage can come from various sources like exposure to the sun, unhealthy habits, or simply the wear and tear of living. Research into extending human lifespan involves exploring ways to slow down or repair this damage. Scientists study things like genetics, diet, and lifestyle to understand how they affect the aging process. They also investigate the potential of interventions like drugs or therapies that could promote healthier aging.

While there have been advances in understanding the biology of aging, extending human lifespan significantly is a complex challenge. The goal isn't just to make people live longer but to ensure those extra years are spent in good health.

In simple terms, scientists are like detectives, trying to uncover the secrets of aging and find ways to help people live longer, healthier lives. While there's no magic solution yet, ongoing research offers hope for advancements that could contribute to extending our lifespan and improving the quality of our later years. It's a journey toward healthier aging and a quest to unravel the mysteries of longevity.

QUESTION 34

What caused the sudden disappearance of the Mayan civilization, and what knowledge and advancements were lost during this enigmatic event?

The sudden disappearance of the Mayan civilization is a historical mystery that researchers have been trying to understand. The story involves exploring the factors behind this enigmatic event and considering the knowledge and advancements that might have been lost.

The Mayan civilization thrived in Mesoamerica for centuries, creating impressive cities, complex calendars, and sophisticated artworks. However, around the 9th century AD, many of their cities were abandoned, and the civilization as a whole declined. Several factors might have contributed to the collapse of the Mayan civilization. One possibility is environmental stress, such as prolonged droughts that could have affected agriculture and water sources. Another factor could be social and political issues, including conflicts, overpopulation, or the breakdown of political systems.

Understanding the specific reasons is challenging because the Maya didn't leave clear explanations. Much of their knowledge was recorded in intricate hieroglyphs, but a lot of these writings have been lost over time due to factors like decay and Spanish colonization.

The collapse of the Mayan civilization meant the loss of valuable knowledge in various fields. The Mayans were skilled astronomers, mathematicians, and builders. Their understanding of the cosmos, advanced agricultural techniques, and intricate artwork were part of the cultural heritage that faced a decline.

While the Mayan civilization experienced a decline, it's important to note that some Mayan cities continued to exist, and the descendants of the ancient Mayans still live in the region today. Modern archaeology and ongoing research efforts continue to uncover the secrets of the Mayan civilization, contributing to a better understanding of their achievements and the factors that led to their decline. It's like solving a historical puzzle, piecing together the story of a once-thriving civilization and the events that shaped its mysterious disappearance.

QUESTION 35

Is there a solution to the long-standing puzzle of the Bermuda Triangle, explaining the mysterious disappearances of ships and planes in that region?

The Bermuda Triangle has been a source of mystery and speculation for a long time, but there isn't a widely accepted scientific solution to the supposed disappearances of ships and planes in that region. The story involves examining the facts and dispelling some myths surrounding the Bermuda Triangle.

Firstly, the Bermuda Triangle is an area in the western part of the North Atlantic Ocean, roughly bound by points in Miami, Bermuda, and Puerto Rico. It gained a reputation for mysterious disappearances due to various incidents reported over the years.

Scientists and experts generally argue that the Bermuda Triangle doesn't have any unusual rate of disappearances compared to other heavily traveled regions of the world. They point out that the area has a high volume of ship and air traffic, which might explain the relatively higher number of incidents.

Some popular theories about the Bermuda Triangle involve natural explanations like underwater features, magnetic anomalies, or methane hydrate eruptions. However, many of these theories lack scientific support, and there's no conclusive evidence that the Bermuda Triangle poses a higher risk than other parts of the ocean.

In simple terms, the Bermuda Triangle mystery is more likely a combination of natural factors, human error, and the exaggeration of incidents over time. While the Bermuda Triangle captures the imagination, the scientific community generally views it as a region with normal navigational challenges and incidents, similar to other busy maritime areas. The search for a definitive solution continues, but as of now, there's no clear evidence supporting the existence of paranormal or mysterious forces in the Bermuda Triangle.

QUESTION 36

How do memories form, and can we pinpoint the physical processes in the brain that encode, store, and retrieve these complex cognitive structures?

The formation of memories is a dynamic process involving encoding, storage, and retrieval in the brain. When we encounter something new, like a friend's face or a fun experience, our brain encodes the details into a memory by creating connections between neurons. These connections, called synapses, play a crucial role in the storage of memories. The hippocampus, a key brain region, helps consolidate information before sending it to other areas for long-term storage. Retrieving a memory involves activating the same neural pathways that were active during encoding, bringing the memory back to our conscious awareness. Scientists use brain imaging and studies of brain-injured patients to understand the role of neurons, synapses, and neurotransmitters in these intricate processes, unraveling the mysteries of how our brain forms and retrieves memories.

While significant progress has been made, the complete understanding of memory formation remains a work in progress. It's akin to exploring the intricate architecture of a complex information storage system within our remarkable brain, where each new discovery adds to the evolving story of how we remember and recall our experiences.

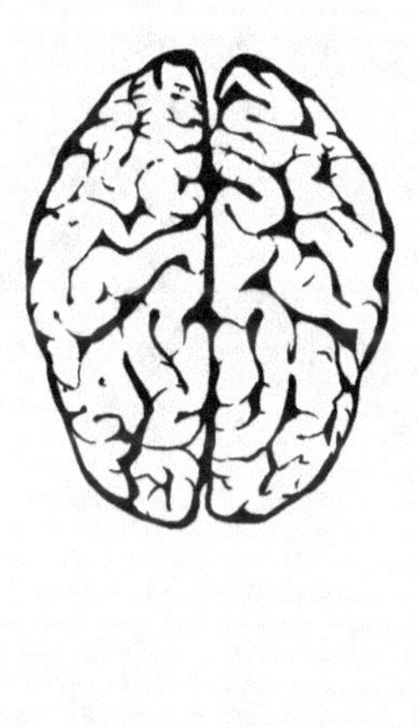

QUESTION 37

Can we understand the origin and purpose of the Nazca Lines, the enormous geoglyphs etched into the Peruvian desert, and the civilization that created them?

The Nazca Lines are enormous drawings etched into the desert floor in Peru, and they've puzzled people for a long time. The story of understanding these geoglyphs involves exploring their origin and purpose, as well as the civilization that created them. The Nazca Lines consist of various shapes, including animals, plants, and geometric patterns, drawn by removing the reddish-brown iron oxide-coated pebbles on the surface to reveal the light-colored earth underneath. Created by the Nazca people, who lived in the region from about 200 BCE to 600 CE, these lines cover a large area and are best seen from above.

Researchers believe that the Nazca Lines served multiple purposes. Some of the figures align with astronomical events, suggesting a connection to celestial calendars or rituals. Others might have been part of religious ceremonies, pilgrimage routes, or even symbols representing water and fertility in this arid region. Despite these theories, the exact purpose remains uncertain as the Nazca people left no written records, and the mystery adds to the fascination of these ancient geoglyphs. Ongoing research and technological advancements, such as satellite imagery, continue to contribute to our understanding of the Nazca Lines, but the full story of their origin and purpose remains a captivating archaeological puzzle.

QUESTION 38

What are the underlying causes of mass extinctions throughout Earth's history, and can we predict and prevent future catastrophic events that could threaten biodiversity?

Mass extinctions in Earth's history have been caused by various factors, and scientists have studied these events to understand their underlying causes. The story involves exploring natural disasters and changes that led to the loss of many species. While predicting and preventing future catastrophic events is challenging, scientists are working to identify potential threats to biodiversity.

One major cause of mass extinctions is asteroid or comet impacts. The most famous example is the impact that likely led to the extinction of dinosaurs around 66 million years ago. The collision released huge amounts of dust and debris, blocking sunlight and disrupting ecosystems.

Another factor is volcanic activity. Massive volcanic eruptions can release vast amounts of lava, gases, and ash, altering the climate and causing environmental changes. The Permian-Triassic extinction, around 252 million years ago, is linked to extensive volcanic activity.

Changes in sea levels and climate have also played a role. During certain mass extinctions, the Earth experienced significant shifts in temperature and sea levels, affecting habitats and ecosystems.

While predicting specific catastrophic events is challenging, scientists are monitoring potential threats, such as near-Earth objects, and developing strategies to minimize risks. Understanding the causes of past extinctions helps researchers identify patterns and potential warning signs. Conservation efforts, environmental protection, and global cooperation are essential to safeguard biodiversity and reduce human impact on the planet. It's like learning from Earth's history to work towards a future where we can better coexist with our planet and its diverse life forms.

QUESTION 39

Is there a limit to the complexity and depth of mathematical structures, or can we continue to uncover new mathematical truths that challenge our understanding of reality ?

The story of mathematics is like an ongoing adventure, and it seems there's no limit to the complexity and depth of mathematical structures. Mathematicians explore abstract ideas and create new concepts, continuously uncovering truths that challenge our understanding of reality.

Mathematics starts with basic ideas, like numbers and shapes, and then builds on these to create more complex structures. As mathematicians dive deeper, they discover unexpected connections and patterns. For example, the exploration of numbers led to the discovery of complex numbers, which include imaginary parts not found in everyday counting.

One fascinating area is set theory, which studies collections of objects. Mathematicians, like Georg Cantor, showed that there are different sizes of infinity, a mind-boggling concept challenging our intuitive understanding of numbers. Another example is the field of fractals, where simple patterns repeat at different scales. Benoit Mandelbrot's work on fractals revolutionized how we see and describe complex shapes in nature, like coastlines and mountains.

The quest for new mathematical truths is ongoing. Mathematicians are tackling problems in areas like number theory, topology, and abstract algebra, pushing the boundaries of what we know. The beauty of mathematics lies in its endless exploration, revealing surprises and challenging us to think beyond our everyday understanding. It's like an ever-expanding journey into the heart of abstract ideas, where the thrill of discovery continues to shape our understanding of the mathematical universe.

$$\sin a = \frac{y}{r}$$

$$\cos a = \frac{x}{r}$$

QUESTION 40

Can we decipher the true intentions and messages behind ancient, enigmatic artifacts like the Antikythera Mechanism or the Baghdad Battery?

Deciphering the true intentions and messages behind ancient artifacts like the Antikythera Mechanism and the Baghdad Battery involves a mix of detective work and scientific investigation. These artifacts hold mysteries that researchers have been unraveling to understand their purpose.

1. Antikythera Mechanism: This ancient Greek device, discovered in a shipwreck, turned out to be a complex mechanism with gears and dials. Initially thought to be a simple decorative object, scientists later realized it was an astronomical calculator, likely used to predict celestial events. Researchers used advanced imaging and computer simulations to understand how it worked, revealing its incredible sophistication and challenging our ideas about ancient technology.

2. Baghdad Battery: The Baghdad Battery, found in Iraq, consists of a clay pot, a copper cylinder, and an iron rod. Some suggest it might have been an ancient battery, but its true purpose is debated. Scientists conducted experiments to see if it could generate an electric charge, and while it's possible, the exact function in ancient times remains uncertain. The mystery of the Baghdad Battery prompts questions about the level of scientific knowledge in ancient cultures.

In both cases, researchers use a combination of archaeological findings, scientific experiments, and historical context to piece together the story behind these artifacts. The challenge lies in interpreting the clues left by ancient civilizations and understanding their technological achievements. While we may not have all the answers, the ongoing work sheds light on the ingenuity of ancient people and opens windows into their advanced knowledge and skills. It's like solving historical puzzles, where each discovery adds a piece to the fascinating narrative of human history.

QUESTION 41

What is the underlying cause of the mysterious hum heard in various locations around the world, and can we mitigate or eliminate this persistent auditory phenomenon?

The mysterious hum heard in various locations around the world is a low-frequency sound that some people report hearing, even though it's not detectable by everyone. The hum has been described as a persistent, low-level noise, and its underlying cause remains a subject of investigation.

Scientists have explored several potential sources for the mysterious hum, including natural phenomena like ocean waves, seismic activity, or atmospheric processes. Human-made sources, such as industrial machinery or transportation, are also considered. However, pinpointing a single, consistent cause has proven challenging. Mitigating or eliminating the mysterious hum involves identifying its specific source and finding ways to reduce or eliminate that source. Researchers use specialized equipment and studies to analyze the frequency and characteristics of the hum in different locations. In some cases, community efforts and local authorities work together to address noise pollution and minimize potential sources of the mysterious hum.

The story of understanding the mysterious hum is ongoing, and researchers continue to investigate its origins and potential solutions. While progress has been made, the complex nature of the phenomenon makes it difficult to offer a one-size-fits-all solution. It's like unraveling a persistent auditory mystery, where each clue brings us closer to understanding and addressing the enigmatic hum reported by communities around the world.

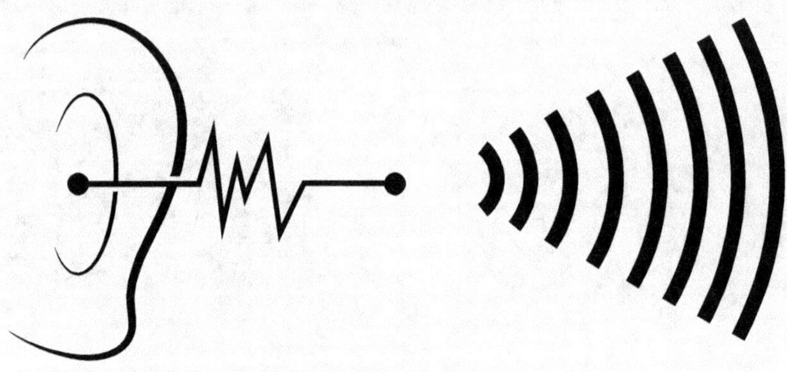

QUESTION 42

Can we uncover the true nature of the so-called "Pioneer anomaly," the unexpected deceleration observed in the trajectories of the Pioneer spacecraft, challenging our understanding of gravitational forces in the outer solar system?

The "Pioneer anomaly" refers to an unexpected slowing down of the Pioneer spacecraft as they moved through the outer solar system. The story of understanding this anomaly involves careful observation, scientific investigation, and the quest to unravel the mystery behind the spacecraft's unexpected behavior.

Scientists initially noticed that the Pioneer spacecraft were not following their expected trajectories as they moved away from the Sun. The anomaly was a tiny but persistent deviation from the predicted paths based on our understanding of gravity. This puzzled researchers because gravitational forces were not acting exactly as anticipated.

The exploration of the Pioneer anomaly involved considering various factors, including the effects of heat emitted by the spacecraft, radiation pressure from the Sun, and even the possibility of unknown forces. Researchers conducted meticulous analyses, taking into account the known forces and factors that could influence the spacecraft's motion.

After much scrutiny, scientists found that thermal radiation from the spacecraft's surfaces—essentially heat emitted by the probes—could explain the observed deviation. The uneven emission of heat created a small force, acting like a gentle push against the direction of motion. This explanation aligned with the observed slowing down of the Pioneer spacecraft.

While the mystery of the Pioneer anomaly has been largely solved, the story reflects the dedication of scientists to understanding unexpected phenomena in space exploration. The meticulous work involved in considering all possible factors, conducting precise measurements, and arriving at a satisfactory explanation showcases the scientific process at its best. It's like solving a cosmic puzzle, where careful analysis and exploration lead to a clearer understanding of the forces shaping our exploration of the outer reaches of the solar system.

QUESTION 43

What is the origin and nature of unidentified flying objects (UFOs), and can we definitively determine whether some represent extraterrestrial technology?

Unidentified Flying Objects (UFOs) are objects or lights in the sky that people observe but cannot immediately identify. The origin and nature of UFOs have been the subject of much speculation and investigation. While many UFO sightings can be explained as natural phenomena, human-made objects, or misinterpretations, some remain unexplained. The story of understanding UFOs involves careful examination by scientists and experts. When people report UFO sightings, investigators try to identify the objects through observations, photographs, and other evidence. Many UFOs turn out to be conventional things like airplanes, weather balloons, or celestial bodies. The challenge lies in cases where the objects cannot be easily identified. Some sightings remain unexplained due to insufficient data, while others might involve classified military activities or technologies. Determining whether UFOs represent extraterrestrial technology is a more complex question. While some people believe that UFOs could be evidence of advanced alien civilizations, the scientific community emphasizes the need for clear and verifiable evidence. UFOs are, by definition, unidentified, and attributing them to extraterrestrial origins requires robust proof.

In recent years, the U.S. government and military have declassified some UFO footage, acknowledging encounters that defy easy explanation. However, this doesn't necessarily confirm extraterrestrial involvement; it highlights the existence of unexplained aerial phenomena.

In simple terms, the study of UFOs involves separating sightings that can be explained from those that remain mysterious. While the possibility of extraterrestrial technology captures the imagination, conclusive evidence is essential for scientific acceptance. The ongoing investigation into UFOs is like a quest for clarity, where researchers strive to differentiate between natural, human-made, and potentially extraordinary phenomena in our skies.

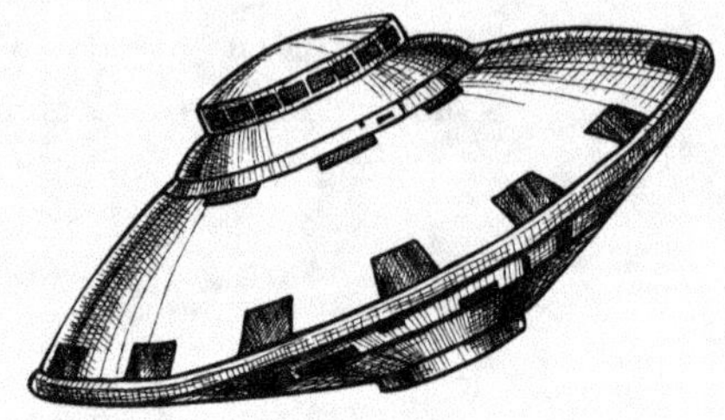

QUESTION 44

Can we prove or disprove the Collatz conjecture, a seemingly simple mathematical problem that has eluded resolution for decades?

The Collatz conjecture is a straightforward mathematical problem that has puzzled mathematicians for a long time. The story of proving or disproving this conjecture involves a seemingly simple rule applied to numbers, yet it has resisted resolution for decades.

The rule of the Collatz conjecture goes like this: Start with any positive integer. If it's even, divide it by 2; if it's odd, multiply it by 3 and add 1. Repeat this process with the resulting number, and the conjecture suggests that, no matter where you start, you'll eventually reach the number 1.

Despite its simplicity, mathematicians have not been able to prove or disprove this conjecture for all numbers. They have tested it extensively using computers, and it holds true for an incredibly large range of starting numbers. However, the challenge lies in proving that it works for every possible starting number.

The Collatz conjecture highlights the beauty and complexity of mathematics. While it appears straightforward, proving its validity for all cases remains an open problem. The story of the Collatz conjecture is ongoing, and mathematicians continue to explore new avenues and techniques in their quest to unlock the secrets behind this seemingly simple yet elusive mathematical puzzle. It's like trying to solve a riddle that teases our understanding of the behavior of numbers in a deceptively simple sequence.

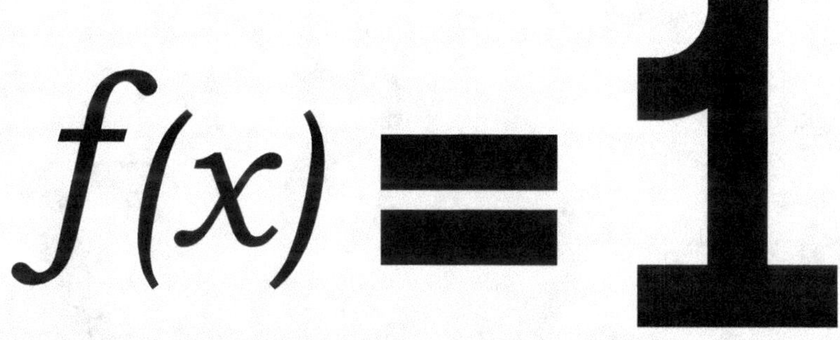

QUESTION 45

Can we determine whether there exist infinitely many twin primes, pairs of primes with a difference of two, as conjectured by the Twin Prime Conjecture?

The Twin Prime Conjecture suggests that there are infinitely many twin primes, which are pairs of prime numbers that have a difference of two (e.g., 11 and 13, or 17 and 19). The story of determining whether this conjecture is true involves the exploration of prime numbers and the quest to find patterns among them.

Primes are numbers greater than 1 that can only be divided evenly by 1 and themselves. Twin primes are pairs of such numbers that have a gap of two between them. Mathematicians have found many twin primes, but the question is whether this pattern continues forever or if there is a largest pair.

The difficulty lies in proving that there are infinitely many twin primes. While mathematicians have discovered large twin prime pairs and identified certain characteristics that twin primes share, proving that they go on forever is a challenging task. The Twin Prime Conjecture remains unproven, and it represents one of the oldest unsolved problems in number theory.

Researchers use advanced mathematical techniques and computer algorithms to explore the distribution of primes and search for evidence supporting or refuting the conjecture. The story of the Twin Prime Conjecture is a tale of mathematical exploration, where mathematicians strive to understand the intricate patterns and behaviors of prime numbers, with the mystery of infinitely many twin primes standing as a captivating challenge yet to be fully resolved. It's like seeking a hidden melody in the sequence of prime numbers, where each new discovery adds a note to the symphony of mathematical understanding.

2 3 5 7

QUESTION 46

Is the mathematical structure of pi (π) truly random, or does it contain hidden patterns that are yet to be discovered?

The mathematical constant pi (π), which represents the ratio of a circle's circumference to its diameter, is known for its seemingly random and never-ending decimal expansion. The story of pi involves exploring whether its digits are truly random or if there are hidden patterns waiting to be discovered.

Mathematicians have calculated pi to trillions of digits and have not found any repeating patterns. The decimals appear to go on forever without a discernible order, which makes pi seem "random." However, randomness in mathematics has a specific meaning, and pi is not considered a truly random number like the outcome of a dice roll.

The mystery lies in whether pi contains hidden patterns beyond what we've discovered so far. Researchers have searched for unusual sequences or occurrences within the digits of pi, and some interesting patterns have been found. For example, certain digit strings may appear more frequently than expected by chance.

The story of pi continues as mathematicians use advanced computational methods to explore its properties. The search for hidden patterns is ongoing, and the fascination with pi lies in its elusive nature. While pi's decimals may not follow a predictable pattern, the exploration of its mathematical structure reflects the never-ending quest for deeper understanding and uncovering surprises within the world of numbers. It's like navigating a vast and uncharted mathematical landscape, where pi stands as a captivating and enigmatic landmark.

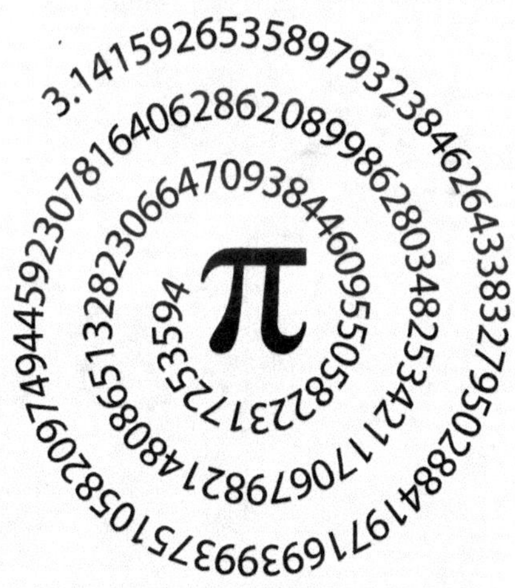

QUESTION 47

Can we find a formula that generates all prime numbers, simplifying the understanding of these fundamental building blocks of arithmetic?

Finding a formula that generates all prime numbers is a challenging and open problem in mathematics. While primes are fundamental building blocks of arithmetic, their distribution appears quite intricate, and no simple formula has been discovered to generate all prime numbers.

The story of this quest involves centuries of mathematical exploration. Primes are numbers greater than 1 that can only be divided evenly by 1 and themselves. They play a crucial role in number theory, yet their pattern isn't easily captured by a straightforward formula.

Early attempts were made to find formulas that generate primes, such as the famous Sieve of Eratosthenes, which can identify primes up to a certain limit. However, a formula that works for all primes, regardless of size, remains elusive.

In the 20th century, mathematicians proved groundbreaking results like the Prime Number Theorem, which gives insights into the distribution of primes but doesn't provide a simple formula for generating them.

Efforts to find such a formula are ongoing, and researchers explore various approaches, including algebraic and analytical methods. The mystery of primes is deeply connected to the nature of numbers, and while no universal formula has been found yet, the quest continues. The story of searching for a formula to generate all prime numbers is like a persistent exploration, where each attempt adds a chapter to the ongoing narrative of understanding the fascinating properties of these essential mathematical entities.

$$x = \frac{-b \pm \sqrt{b^2 - 4ac}}{2a}$$

$$ax^2 + bx + c = 0$$

QUESTION 48

Is it possible to construct a three-dimensional analogue of a perfect sphere in higher dimensions, addressing the curious and challenging Banach-Tarski paradox?

The Banach-Tarski paradox is a mind-bending concept in mathematics that deals with the idea of dividing a mathematical object, like a sphere, into a finite number of pieces and rearranging them to create two identical copies of the original. This paradox challenges our intuition and understanding of space and shapes.

In simple terms, the paradox suggests that it's possible to take a sphere, split it into a finite number of non-overlapping pieces, and then reassemble those pieces to create two identical spheres, each the same size as the original.

The construction involves abstract mathematical concepts and doesn't have a direct physical counterpart. It relies on the properties of mathematical objects in higher-dimensional spaces. The paradox doesn't violate the laws of physics; instead, it highlights the weird and counterintuitive nature of certain mathematical ideas.

The Banach-Tarski paradox is not practical in the physical world; it's more of a theoretical concept that explores the unusual properties of infinite-dimensional spaces. While it might seem puzzling, the paradox doesn't lead to real-world applications or the creation of infinite copies of physical objects. It's a fascinating example of how mathematical thinking can sometimes challenge our everyday understanding of space and reality.

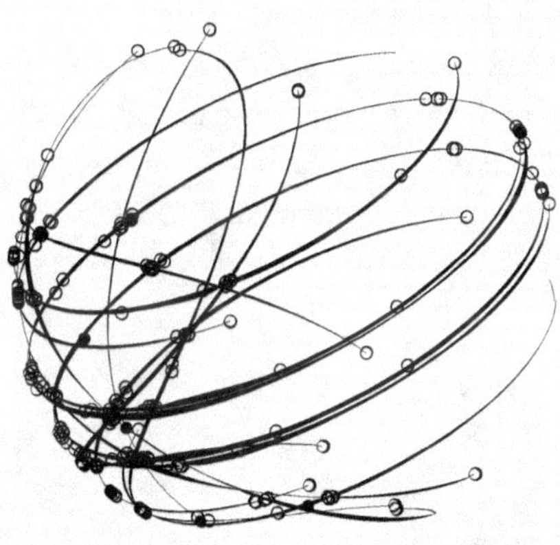

QUESTION 49

Can we uncover the complete story behind infamous sporting controversies, like the Black Sox Scandal or the Tonya Harding and Nancy Kerrigan incident?

1. **Black Sox Scandal (1919):** The Black Sox Scandal revolves around the 1919 World Series in baseball. The Chicago White Sox were accused of intentionally losing the championship to the Cincinnati Reds in exchange for money from gamblers. Eight players, known as the "Black Sox," were banned from baseball for life. The scandal exposed corruption in the sport and led to reforms in baseball governance. Investigations revealed that some players had agreed to throw the games, tarnishing the integrity of the World Series. The aftermath saw baseball implement strict rules against gambling to protect the fairness and honesty of the game.

2. **Tonya Harding and Nancy Kerrigan Incident (1994):** The Tonya Harding and Nancy Kerrigan incident was a figure skating controversy during the 1994 U.S. Figure Skating Championships. Tonya Harding's ex-husband hired someone to attack Nancy Kerrigan, a rival skater, injuring her knee. The motive was to eliminate Kerrigan as competition for Harding. The incident shocked the sports world and gained widespread media attention. Harding pleaded guilty to hindering the prosecution of the attackers but maintained she had no knowledge of the plot beforehand. The scandal resulted in Harding's ban from competitive figure skating and further scrutiny of ethics in sports.

Both controversies reveal the darker side of sports, involving cheating, corruption, and criminal actions. These incidents not only impacted the athletes involved but also prompted changes in the way sports are managed and regulated, emphasizing the importance of fair play, ethics, and integrity in the world of athletics. The stories serve as cautionary tales, reminding us of the ongoing efforts to uphold the principles that make sports a fair and honorable pursuit.

QUESTION 50

Can we definitively identify the historical figure or figures behind the legend of Robin Hood, separating fact from fiction?

Identifying the historical figure behind the legend of Robin Hood is a challenging task, as the story of Robin Hood has evolved over centuries and is deeply rooted in folklore. The legend of Robin Hood depicts a heroic outlaw who robs from the rich to give to the poor, living in Sherwood Forest with his band of Merry Men. While the legend is beloved, separating fact from fiction is complicated.

Several historical figures have been suggested as potential inspirations for Robin Hood, but there is no conclusive evidence to pinpoint a single individual. Some theories propose that Robin Hood is an amalgamation of various outlaws or that the character represents a symbolic figure embodying resistance against oppression. The lack of historical records and the blending of folklore with real historical events make it challenging to definitively identify the true Robin Hood. The legend has been passed down through ballads, stories, and plays, contributing to its enduring popularity.

In essence, the story of Robin Hood remains a captivating mystery, where the line between historical fact and legendary fiction is blurred. While we may never uncover a single historical figure behind the legend, the enduring appeal of Robin Hood lies in the timeless themes of justice, heroism, and the fight against tyranny that continue to resonate with audiences around the world.

QUESTION 51

Can we definitively identify the mysterious historical figure known as the **Man in the Iron Mask**, and what secrets might his identity reveal about European history?

The Man in the Iron Mask is a mysterious historical figure whose identity remains uncertain, sparking various theories and speculations. The story involves a prisoner in France during the late 17th century who was forced to wear an iron mask, and his true identity has been a subject of intrigue and debate.

Historical records and accounts provide glimpses into the life of the Man in the Iron Mask, but his identity has never been definitively established. Various theories suggest that he could have been a high-profile political prisoner, a royal twin, or even a secret sibling of King Louis XIV.

The mystery of the Man in the Iron Mask has inspired literature, movies, and countless discussions. The true identity, however, continues to elude historians, and the secrets his story might reveal about European history remain shrouded in uncertainty.

Unraveling the mystery of the Man in the Iron Mask involves sifting through historical records, examining political contexts, and considering the intrigues of the time. While the true identity may never be conclusively determined, the enigma surrounding this figure adds a layer of mystique to European history, prompting ongoing fascination and speculation. It's like solving a historical puzzle, where each clue offers a glimpse into the complex tapestry of 17th-century Europe, leaving some aspects forever veiled in mystery.

QUESTION 52

Can we definitively identify the historical figure or figures responsible for the construction of Stonehenge, uncovering the purpose and methods behind this ancient monument?

The construction of Stonehenge, an ancient monument in England, remains a historical mystery, and definitively identifying the individuals responsible is challenging. Stonehenge is a circle of standing stones, some weighing tons, arranged in a specific pattern, and it dates back to around 3000 BCE. The story of understanding Stonehenge involves archaeological investigations and numerous theories. Archaeologists believe that the construction took place over several phases, with the earliest phase involving the digging of circular ditches and the placement of wooden posts. The iconic standing stones came later, and their transportation and arrangement continue to intrigue scholars.

Several theories about Stonehenge's purpose exist. Some believe it served as an astronomical observatory or a religious site, while others suggest it had ceremonial or burial functions. The methods used to transport and position the massive stones are also subjects of speculation, with possibilities ranging from sledges and rollers to more complex engineering solutions.

The story of Stonehenge's exploration involves a combination of archaeological digs, scientific analysis, and historical research. While there are intriguing clues about its purpose and construction, the monument's full story remains partially veiled in the mists of ancient history.

In simple terms, Stonehenge's construction involves a mix of mystery and scientific inquiry. Theories abound, but the exact details and purpose remain elusive, adding to the allure of this ancient monument and leaving room for ongoing exploration and discovery.

QUESTION 53

Can we uncover the true nature of the so-called "Great Filter," a hypothetical concept that may explain why advanced extraterrestrial civilizations are seemingly rare or absent in the observable universe?

The "Great Filter" is a hypothetical concept in the search for extraterrestrial intelligence (SETI) that suggests there might be some challenging step or obstacle that makes it difficult for life to evolve into advanced civilizations. This could explain why we haven't yet observed or communicated with other advanced extraterrestrial civilizations in the vast universe.

The story of the Great Filter involves considering the different stages that life might go through, from simple single-celled organisms to complex, intelligent civilizations. The idea is that at some point in this process, there is a "filter" that significantly reduces the chances of progressing to the next stage. This filter could be a rare and difficult-to-achieve step, such as the emergence of intelligent life or the ability to communicate over long distances.

If the Great Filter is behind us, it means that life faces significant challenges in evolving into intelligent civilizations. If it lies ahead of us, it suggests that advanced civilizations might be rare because they face a difficult hurdle that most do not overcome.

Scientists use the Great Filter concept to explore the possible reasons for the apparent absence of observable advanced extraterrestrial civilizations. It's like trying to figure out where in the process of evolution advanced civilizations might face a significant challenge, and this challenge could be one reason why we haven't encountered other intelligent beings in the vast cosmos. The true nature of the Great Filter remains speculative, but the concept encourages us to think deeply about the conditions that lead to the emergence and survival of intelligent life in the universe.

QUESTION 54

What is the mechanism behind the formation of supermassive black holes at the centers of galaxies?

The formation of supermassive black holes at the centers of galaxies is a captivating process that unfolds in cosmic scales. It begins with the existence of smaller black holes, known as "seed" black holes, which originate from the remnants of massive stars undergoing gravitational collapse. These initial black holes serve as the starting point for the growth of supermassive black holes.

As the story progresses, these seed black holes start to accumulate mass through accretion, pulling in nearby gas and dust. This process intensifies as galaxies themselves collide and merge. When galaxies merge, the black holes at their centers can also merge, forming a larger black hole with an increasing mass.

The journey towards supermassive black holes continues as these cosmic giants reach millions or even billions of times the mass of our Sun. Their influence becomes significant, and the feeding and merging processes at the galactic centers contribute to the evolution of both the black holes and their host galaxies.

This growth is often accompanied by intense activity, observed as an "Active Galactic Nucleus" (AGN), where the supermassive black hole releases tremendous energy in the form of light. The AGN's influence on the surrounding galaxy plays a crucial role in shaping the galactic environment.

Scientists use powerful telescopes and instruments to study these complex processes, uncovering the mysteries of supermassive black holes and their impact on the cosmic structures they inhabit. While our understanding has grown significantly, the story of supermassive black hole formation remains a dynamic field of exploration, reminding us of the vastness and intricacy of the universe.

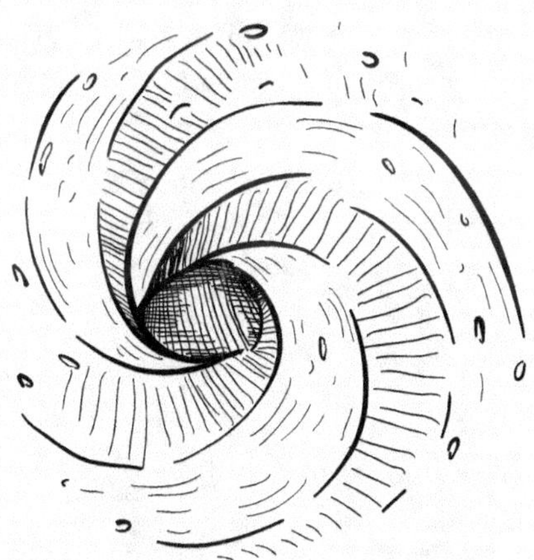

QUESTION 55

What is the true nature of the "great attractor" influencing the motion of galaxies in our cosmic neighborhood?

The "Great Attractor" is a mysterious cosmic force that influences the motion of galaxies in our cosmic neighborhood. To understand its nature, let's dive into the story of the works on this intriguing phenomenon in simple terms.

As astronomers observed the motion of galaxies in the universe, they noticed that they were not moving as expected based on the gravitational pull of visible matter alone. Something else, something massive and hidden from direct observation, seemed to be tugging on these galaxies.

Scientists proposed that there exists a massive concentration of matter, including galaxies and dark matter, that exerts a gravitational force strong enough to affect the motion of nearby galaxies. This unseen force acts like a cosmic magnet, drawing galaxies toward it.

The challenge lies in directly observing the Great Attractor because it is located in a region of the sky obscured by the Milky Way's dust and stars. This makes it difficult to get a clear view using visible light observations.

To uncover its secrets, astronomers use alternative methods like studying the motion of galaxies and mapping the distribution of mass in our cosmic neighborhood. While the exact nature of the Great Attractor remains somewhat enigmatic, it represents a critical aspect of the cosmic web, the vast structure of galaxies and dark matter that forms the backbone of the universe.

In essence, the story of the Great Attractor involves detecting the subtle gravitational influences on nearby galaxies, pointing to an unseen concentration of mass with a significant impact on the large-scale structure of our cosmic neighborhood. The ongoing quest to unveil the true nature of the Great Attractor continues to captivate astronomers and deepen our understanding of the cosmic forces shaping the universe.

QUESTION 56

What is the true nature of the "great attractor" influencing the motion of galaxies in our cosmic neighborhood?

The Roswell UFO incident in 1947 is a famous event surrounded by controversy and speculation. To understand its true nature and separate fact from fiction, let's break down the story using simple words.

In July 1947, a rancher near Roswell, New Mexico, discovered debris scattered across his land. The U.S. military initially released a statement saying they had recovered a "flying disc," sparking widespread interest in UFOs (Unidentified Flying Objects). However, the military quickly revised its statement, claiming the debris was from a weather balloon.

Over the years, conspiracy theories emerged, suggesting that the government covered up the recovery of an extraterrestrial spacecraft and even alien bodies. Many people believed there was more to the story than the military's official explanation.

Decades later, in the 1990s, the U.S. government declassified documents related to the Roswell incident. These documents supported the military's explanation that the debris was, indeed, from a top-secret project called Project Mogul, which used high-altitude balloons to monitor Soviet nuclear tests.

While the government's explanation is supported by evidence, the Roswell incident remains a topic of debate and fascination. Some still hold onto the idea that there was a UFO cover-up, while others accept the official account. The story of Roswell underscores how narratives can evolve over time and how the quest for the truth often involves sifting through layers of information and speculation.

QUESTION 57

Can we unravel the mysteries surrounding the lost colony of Popham in the early 17th century, predating the Plymouth Colony?

The lost colony of Popham in the early 17th century is a historical mystery that predates the more well-known Plymouth Colony. To understand the story of the works on this enigmatic event, let's use simple words.

In 1607, English settlers established the Popham Colony in present-day Maine, aiming to create a thriving community for trade and settlement. However, the colony's fate became uncertain when some colonists returned to England, possibly due to harsh conditions and challenges.

The mystery deepened when, in 1608, when a supply ship arrived, the settlers discovered the colony deserted. The buildings were empty, and there was no sign of the people who had once lived there. The fate of the Popham Colony remains unclear, and historians have speculated about various possibilities, including conflicts with Native Americans, struggles for survival, or a decision to relocate.

Despite archaeological efforts and historical research, the exact reasons behind the disappearance of the Popham Colony have not been definitively determined. The story reflects the challenges faced by early English attempts at colonization in North America and the mysteries that can linger when historical records are scarce. The lost colony of Popham remains an intriguing chapter in the early history of European settlements in the New World, leaving historians and archaeologists with an ongoing puzzle to solve.

QUESTION 58

Can we determine the identity and motives of the infamous hijacker known as D.B. Cooper, who vanished without a trace in 1971?

The case of D.B. Cooper, the infamous hijacker who vanished without a trace in 1971, is a captivating mystery. Let's explore the story and the efforts to determine his identity and motives in simple terms.

In November 1971, a man using the alias D.B. Cooper hijacked a commercial airplane, demanding ransom money and then parachuting out of the plane, disappearing into thin air. Despite an extensive manhunt and investigations, neither Cooper nor the majority of the ransom money has been definitively found.

The mystery deepens as investigators have considered various theories about Cooper's identity and motives. Some believe he was an experienced skydiver, while others think he had knowledge of the specific aircraft and the terrain where he parachuted.

Numerous suspects have been proposed over the years, but none have been conclusively proven to be D.B. Cooper. The motives behind the hijacking remain speculative, ranging from financial desperation to a carefully planned escape.

The case continues to capture the public's imagination, and the FBI has kept it open, although no major breakthroughs have occurred. The story of D.B. Cooper stands as one of the greatest unsolved mysteries in criminal history, leaving the identity and motives of the hijacker shrouded in mystery and speculation. The search for answers continues, making it a captivating tale of a mysterious disappearance that has puzzled investigators for decades.

QUESTION 59

What was the true cause of the Tunguska event in 1908, which resulted in a massive explosion in Siberia?

In 1908, the Tunguska event shook the remote Siberian landscape with a colossal explosion, flattening vast expanses of forest without leaving a discernible crater. Initially shrouded in mystery, scientists grappled with understanding the cause of this extraordinary event. The prevailing theory emerged, suggesting that a space rock, possibly a comet or asteroid around 50 to 60 meters in diameter, entered Earth's atmosphere and experienced an airburst. The intense heat and pressure generated by the friction with the atmosphere caused the rock to explode before reaching the ground, releasing an energy equivalent to a powerful nuclear blast.

Scientific expeditions to the Tunguska region, despite its challenging terrain, uncovered crucial evidence supporting the space rock hypothesis. The presence of unusual materials and distinctive patterns of scorching on trees near the epicenter added weight to the conclusion that a cosmic intruder had burst into fragments above the Siberian landscape. The Tunguska event stands as a stark reminder of the potential cosmic hazards our planet faces and exemplifies the ongoing efforts to understand and monitor the dynamics between Earth and space.

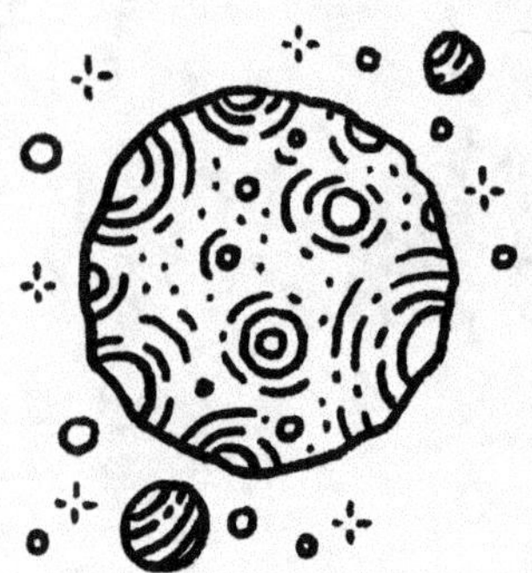

QUESTION 60

How can we determine the precise decimal expansion of mathematical constants like π and e to an infinite number of digits?

Determining the infinite decimal expansion of mathematical constants like π (pi) and e involves clever mathematical techniques and lots of patience. Let's explore the story of how mathematicians work on this using simple words.

π (Pi): Pi is the ratio of a circle's circumference to its diameter. Mathematicians have been fascinated by pi for centuries, and calculating its decimal expansion has been a historical challenge. One method, called the "archimedes method," involves inscribing and circumscribing polygons around a circle to get better and better approximations of pi. Modern approaches, like algorithms and formulas, use computers to calculate pi to millions, billions, or even trillions of digits.

e (Euler's Number): Euler's number, denoted as "e," is a mathematical constant that appears in various areas of mathematics. Calculating its decimal expansion involves understanding its definition as the sum of an infinite series. Mathematicians use calculus and infinite series techniques to express e and compute its digits. Similar to pi, computers play a crucial role in calculating e to a vast number of decimal places.

Techniques and Algorithms: The algorithms used to compute these constants leverage mathematical properties and formulas. Some, like the Bailey–Borwein–Plouffe (BBP) formula for pi, provide a way to calculate specific digits without needing to compute all preceding ones. These methods, combined with the computational power of modern computers, allow mathematicians to uncover more and more digits of these constants.

Applications: While calculating these constants to an infinite number of digits may seem like a mathematical curiosity, it has practical applications in various fields like cryptography, where highly accurate values are needed. Additionally, exploring the patterns in these expansions provides insights into the nature of these mathematical constants.

In essence, the story involves a historical quest to understand and calculate the decimal expansions of mathematical constants using a combination of clever mathematical techniques, algorithms, and the computational power of modern technology. The pursuit of more digits continues to be an ongoing journey in the world of mathematics.

QUESTION 61

Can the P versus NP problem, a fundamental question in computer science and mathematics, be definitively answered?

The P versus NP problem lies at the heart of computer science and mathematics, posing a question that has captivated researchers for decades. In simple terms, it asks whether problems that can be quickly checked for solutions (in polynomial time, denoted as "P") can also be efficiently solved by a computer. The importance of this question is immense, as a positive answer would imply that efficiently verifying solutions to problems is equivalent to finding those solutions efficiently, with profound implications for various fields, including cryptography and algorithmic efficiency.

Despite numerous attempts by brilliant minds in the field, solving the P versus NP problem has proven exceptionally challenging. The difficulty arises from the intricate nature of the question – it's akin to trying to decipher an elaborate puzzle where each potential solution introduces new complexities. The problem's complexity places it among the Millennium Prize Problems, a collection of seven unsolved mathematical challenges, highlighting its significance and the intellectual depth required for its resolution.

The ongoing story of the works on the P versus NP problem reflects the persistence and dedication of mathematicians and computer scientists in unraveling its mysteries. As researchers explore different approaches, develop new mathematical tools, and harness the power of computational techniques, the hope is to one day provide a definitive answer to this fundamental question, reshaping our understanding of computation and problem-solving in the digital age.

QUESTION 62

What is the minimum number of colors required to color any map so that no two adjacent regions have the same color, as stated in the Four Color Theorem?

The Four Color Theorem is a celebrated concept in mathematics that revolves around the challenge of coloring maps without adjacent regions sharing the same color. The central question asks: What is the minimum number of colors required to ensure that no two neighboring regions on a map have the same color? In the case of the Four Color Theorem, the surprising answer is that four colors are always sufficient.

The origins of this theorem trace back to the 19th century when Francis Guthrie, a mathematician, pondered the idea that four colors might be adequate to color any map without conflicts. However, proving this conjecture turned out to be a complex and elusive task. The Four Color Theorem became a historical puzzle that captivated mathematicians for decades, representing one of the classic problems in the field of graph theory.

The breakthrough in proving the Four Color Theorem came in the 1970s with mathematicians Kenneth Appel and Wolfgang Haken. Their proof involved a combination of human insights and computer-assisted verification. Using computers to check an extensive number of cases, they demonstrated that no map requires more than four colors. While some mathematicians prefer purely theoretical proofs, the successful resolution of the Four Color Theorem showcased the synergy between human reasoning and computational tools in tackling intricate mathematical challenges, marking a significant achievement in the realm of graph theory and combinatorics.

QUESTION 63

What governs the origin and behavior of cosmic magnetic fields?

The origin and behavior of cosmic magnetic fields are intriguing aspects of astrophysics, and understanding them involves exploring the story of the works in this field using simple words.

Magnetic Fields in Space: Magnetic fields exist throughout the universe, influencing the behavior of celestial objects like stars, galaxies, and even the vast cosmic gas between them. These fields play a crucial role in shaping the dynamics of cosmic structures.

Formation of Magnetic Fields: The origin of cosmic magnetic fields is not fully understood, but various processes are believed to contribute to their creation. One significant mechanism is the "dynamo effect," where the motion of electrically charged particles generates and amplifies magnetic fields. This process occurs within stars, galaxies, and other cosmic structures.

Stellar Dynamos: Stars, including our Sun, have their own magnetic fields generated by the movement of charged particles in their interiors. The Sun's magnetic activity, seen in phenomena like sunspots and solar flares, is a result of its dynamo process. Similarly, other stars exhibit magnetic behaviors influenced by their internal processes.

Galactic Magnetic Fields: Galaxies also harbor magnetic fields, and their origins are tied to the interplay of various astrophysical processes. The movement of cosmic gas, the rotation of galaxies, and the interactions between magnetic fields and cosmic rays contribute to the complexity of galactic magnetic structures.

Cosmic Evolution: Understanding the evolution of cosmic magnetic fields involves studying the interstellar medium, cosmic plasma, and the life cycles of stars and galaxies. Magnetic fields play a vital role in regulating star formation, galactic structure, and even the behavior of cosmic jets emanating from black holes.

In essence, the story of cosmic magnetic fields is an intricate tale of dynamo processes, charged particles in motion, and the influence of magnetic fields on the evolution and behavior of celestial objects. While many details remain to be unraveled, astronomers continue to probe the cosmos to deepen our understanding of these captivating cosmic forces.

QUESTION 64

Can we gain a comprehensive understanding of the motives and circumstances surrounding the assassination of President John F. Kennedy in 1963?

The assassination of President John F. Kennedy in 1963 is a pivotal and enduringly mysterious event in American history. On that fateful day in Dallas, Texas, Kennedy was shot while riding in a motorcade, leading to a series of investigations and inquiries. The official investigation, led by the Warren Commission, concluded that Lee Harvey Oswald acted alone, firing shots from the Texas School Book Depository. However, the abrupt killing of Oswald by Jack Ruby only two days later added a layer of intrigue and suspicion.

Despite the Warren Commission's findings, the assassination has been shrouded in conspiracy theories, suggesting that Oswald may not have acted in isolation. Various alternative theories implicated organized crime, the CIA, or other political entities.

The lack of a clear motive for Oswald's actions and the mysterious circumstances surrounding his arrest and subsequent death fueled doubts and suspicions, giving rise to a persistent public quest for answers.

Subsequent investigations, such as the House Select Committee on Assassinations in the 1970s, revisited the case and acknowledged the possibility of a conspiracy without definitively proving one. The assassination of President Kennedy remains a subject of intense public interest, with ongoing debates, numerous investigations, and a wealth of cultural interpretations seeking to unravel the motives and circumstances behind this tragic and historic event. Despite decades of scrutiny, a comprehensive understanding that satisfies all remains elusive, contributing to the enduring mystery of JFK's assassination.

QUESTION 65

How did the ancient city of Troy fall, and to what extent does the Trojan War described in mythology align with historical events?

The story of the fall of Troy is a legendary tale that weaves together mythology and historical elements. In Greek mythology, the Trojan War is sparked by the abduction of Helen, the wife of a Greek king, Paris, a Trojan prince. This event leads to a protracted conflict between the Greeks and the Trojans. The war is filled with epic heroes such as Achilles and Agamemnon, and it culminates in the famous ruse of the Trojan Horse. The Greeks, unable to breach Troy's walls through traditional means, pretend to retreat and leave a massive wooden horse as a supposed peace offering. The Trojans bring the horse into their city, not realizing that Greek soldiers hidden inside would emerge at night to open the gates for the Greek army, resulting in the fall of Troy.

Archaeological excavations at the ancient site of Troy, led by Heinrich Schliemann in the late 19th century, added a layer of historical credibility to the myth. The remains of Troy, identified as multiple layers corresponding to different periods, showed signs of destruction around the time traditionally associated with the Trojan War. While the archaeological evidence doesn't perfectly align with every detail of the myth, it suggests that Troy was a real city that faced significant upheaval, possibly due to conflict.

The blending of myth and history in the fall of Troy showcases the complex relationship between legendary narratives and archaeological discoveries. The story has endured for centuries, capturing the imagination of people around the world, and the ongoing debate about the extent to which the Trojan War aligns with historical events continues to fuel scholarly discussions and public fascination.

QUESTION 66

How did the legendary city of Pompeii meet its end during the eruption of Mount Vesuvius in 79 AD, and what insights can it provide into daily life in ancient Rome?

The destruction of the legendary city of Pompeii unfolded during the catastrophic eruption of Mount Vesuvius in 79 AD. The volcano unleashed a violent eruption, sending ash, pumice, and debris raining down on Pompeii and nearby Herculaneum. While Herculaneum faced the immediate impact of hot pyroclastic flows, Pompeii experienced a slower burial as layers of ash blanketed the city. This sudden catastrophe buried the thriving Roman city, freezing it in time and preserving its structures and artifacts.

Centuries later, in the 18th century, the rediscovery and subsequent excavations of Pompeii unveiled an extraordinary archaeological site. The layers of ash acted as a natural preservative, revealing an astonishingly well-preserved snapshot of daily life in ancient Rome. Streets, homes, public buildings, and even human remains were uncovered, providing modern scholars with a unique opportunity to study various aspects of Roman culture, including architecture, urban planning, social structures, and economic activities.

Among the poignant findings were the plaster casts of human voids created by the ash. These casts preserved the shapes and poses of the residents of Pompeii at the moment of their demise. These haunting imprints offer a visceral connection to the people who lived in the city, immortalizing the tragic and abrupt end they faced during the eruption of Mount Vesuvius. In essence, the story of Pompeii is a testament to the enduring power of natural disasters and their ability to both devastate and preserve the echoes of ancient civilizations.

QUESTION 67

What causes the occasional involuntary muscle twitch, or "myoclonic jerk," particularly when falling asleep, and can we understand the triggers behind this phenomenon?

 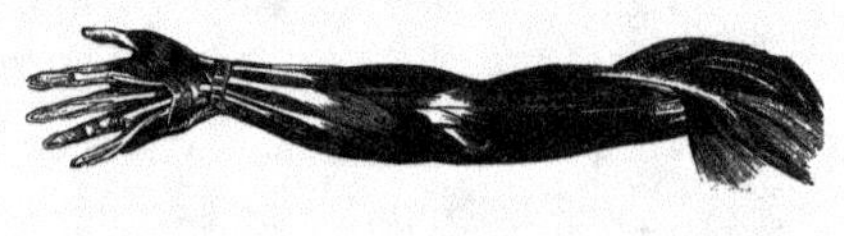

The mystery behind the occasional involuntary muscle twitch, known as a myoclonic jerk, particularly when falling asleep, is a common and intriguing phenomenon. This mysterious muscle movement has its roots in the complex interplay between the brain and the body during the transitional state between wakefulness and sleep. As individuals drift into sleep, their brains undergo various changes in activity, leading to shifts in muscle tone and coordination.

The story begins with the stages of sleep, specifically the transition from wakefulness to the initial phases of light sleep. During this transition, the brain experiences changes in electrical activity, and the muscles undergo a process called hypnic jerks. These jerks or twitches are thought to be a natural part of the body's relaxation process as it prepares for deeper sleep. While the exact triggers for these jerks aren't fully understood, they are believed to be linked to the abrupt transition between wakefulness and sleep, causing a momentary miscommunication in the nervous system.

This mystery deepens when considering potential factors that may contribute to the frequency and intensity of these myoclonic jerks. Stress, caffeine consumption, and irregular sleep patterns are among the factors that could influence the likelihood of experiencing these twitches. While researchers have made strides in understanding the general mechanisms behind hypnic jerks, the specific nuances of individual experiences and the variability in triggers contribute to the ongoing enigma surrounding this common and often harmless phenomenon.

QUESTION 68

Can we uncover the true identity of the elusive serial killer known as Jack the Ripper, who terrorized London in the late 19th century?

The tale of Jack the Ripper, the notorious serial killer who struck fear into the heart of Victorian London during 1888, is a perplexing and unsolved mystery. The murders took place in the Whitechapel district, where several women fell victim to a brutal assailant. The killer, dubbed Jack the Ripper, earned notoriety for the gruesomeness of the crimes and the apparent ease with which he eluded capture. The name itself was popularized through letters sent to a London newspaper, fueling both terror and fascination.

The investigations into the Jack the Ripper case were marked by the challenges of the time, including the absence of modern forensic methods and a lack of conclusive evidence. Despite the efforts of the police and various theories proposed over the years, the true identity of Jack the Ripper remains elusive. Theories range from local suspects to more sensational claims, but none have been definitively proven.

The legacy of Jack the Ripper persists in popular culture, with ongoing public fascination and numerous attempts by amateur sleuths and historians to solve the mystery. The case has become a symbol of the difficulty in uncovering historical crimes, especially those shrouded in the passage of time and limited available evidence. Jack the Ripper's identity continues to be a haunting enigma, leaving a chilling mark on the annals of criminal history.

QUESTION 69

Can we decipher the complete map of neural connectivity in the human brain, known as the "connectome"?

Deciphering the complete connectome, the intricate network of neural connections in the human brain, is a scientific quest at the intersection of neuroscience, technology, and computation. Researchers employ sophisticated brain imaging techniques, such as Magnetic Resonance Imaging (MRI) and Diffusion Tensor Imaging (DTI), to visualize the brain's structure and map the pathways connecting its billions of neurons. These methods provide snapshots of the brain's anatomy, revealing white matter tracts and aiding in the reconstruction of the connectome.

The challenge lies in the vast complexity of the human brain. The connectome represents an intricate tapestry of neural connections, influencing everything from basic sensory functions to higher-order cognitive processes. Scientists face the formidable task of not only mapping these connections but also understanding their functional significance. Ongoing research involves the development of more advanced imaging technologies, computational models, and collaborative efforts to uncover the complexities of the connectome.

While significant progress has been made in mapping specific aspects of neural connectivity, achieving a comprehensive and detailed connectome remains an ongoing endeavor. The continuous advancement of technology, coupled with interdisciplinary collaboration, brings us closer to unraveling the secrets of how different regions of the brain communicate and coordinate. The story of the connectome unfolds as a testament to the boundless intricacies of the human brain, promising profound insights into cognition, behavior, and neurological disorders.

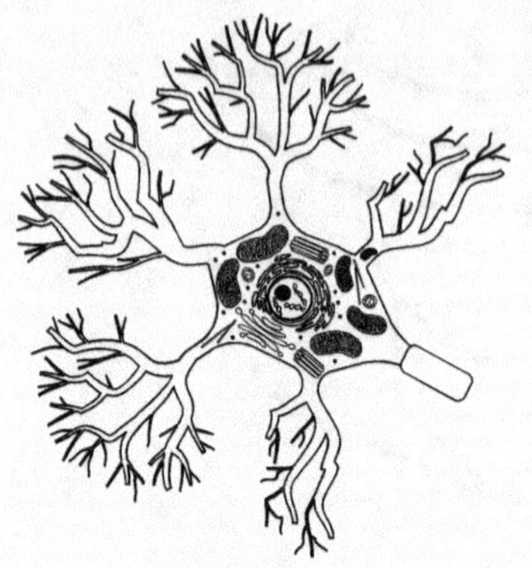 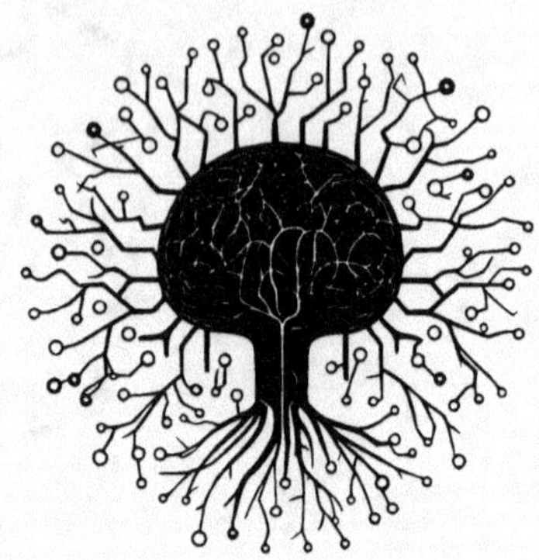

QUESTION 70

What are the secrets behind iconic artworks like the Mona Lisa or The Starry Night?

The Mona Lisa, crafted by Leonardo da Vinci in the early 16th century, harbors its secrets in da Vinci's pioneering artistic techniques. The mysterious smile and captivating gaze of the subject, Lisa Gherardini, are brought to life through da Vinci's use of sfumato. This method involves blending colors seamlessly, creating a soft transition between light and shadow. The subtle nuances in the Mona Lisa's expression, combined with da Vinci's meticulous attention to the play of light on her face, contribute to the painting's timeless allure. The painting's enduring mystery lies not only in the subject's enigmatic smile but also in da Vinci's mastery of techniques that have left an indelible mark on art history.

Vincent van Gogh's The Starry Night, painted in 1889, holds its own set of secrets. Van Gogh's emotionally charged masterpiece, created during his stay in an asylum, captures the swirling night sky with vivid colors and dynamic brushstrokes. The painting's emotional intensity is conveyed through van Gogh's bold use of color and the unique texture achieved with the impasto technique. The swirling patterns in the sky and the prominent cypress tree in the foreground are believed to reflect van Gogh's inner turmoil. The Starry Night, with its distinctive blend of vibrant colors and expressive style, stands as a testament to van Gogh's emotional depth and has become an iconic representation of his artistic genius.

In conclusion, the secrets behind these iconic artworks lie not only in the skillful techniques employed by da Vinci and van Gogh but also in the personal stories and emotional depth that infuse the paintings with enduring appeal. The Mona Lisa's mysterious allure and The Starry Night's emotional intensity continue to captivate and inspire art enthusiasts around the world, showcasing the timeless power of these masterpieces.

QUESTION 71

Can we uncover the real story behind the mystery of Anastasia Romanov's survival or demise during the Russian Revolution?

The mystery surrounding Anastasia Romanov's fate during the Russian Revolution is a complex and intriguing tale that has captivated historians and the public for decades. Anastasia was the youngest daughter of Tsar Nicholas II, the last Russian monarch. In 1918, during the Russian Revolution, the Romanov family was imprisoned and later executed by Bolsheviks. For many years, the fate of Anastasia and her brother Alexei remained uncertain.

In 1991, a breakthrough occurred when the remains of the Romanov family were discovered in a mass grave in Ekaterinburg, Russia. However, the mystery deepened as two bodies were missing—those of Anastasia and Alexei. In 2007, additional remains were found in a separate grave, about 70 kilometers away. DNA testing confirmed the identity of Anastasia and Alexei, providing conclusive evidence of their demise. The discovery brought closure to the long-standing mystery and confirmed that Anastasia Romanov did not survive the tragic events of the Russian Revolution.

Anastasia's story has been further popularized by various myths and impostors who claimed to be her. The enduring mystery surrounding her fate, fueled by rumors and misinformation, eventually found resolution through scientific advancements and the discovery of the Romanov family's remains. The tragic fate of Anastasia and her family stands as a poignant chapter in history, reflecting the tumultuous times of the Russian Revolution and the eventual unraveling of the mystery that surrounded their deaths.

QUESTION 72

What happened to the 3 guys who escaped from Alcatraz?

The escape from Alcatraz, one of the most famous prison breaks in history, occurred in 1962 when three inmates—Frank Morris and brothers John and Clarence Anglin—managed to break out of the maximum-security prison on Alcatraz Island. The escape involved an elaborate plan that took months to devise. The trio crafted makeshift life vests and a makeshift raft using raincoats, and they used spoons and a drill made from a vacuum cleaner motor to create holes in their cells' vent openings.

On the night of June 11, 1962, Morris and the Anglin brothers executed their plan. They crawled through the holes they had made, reached the roof, and descended to the ground using a utility corridor. From there, they inflated their makeshift raft and paddled away into the dark waters of San Francisco Bay. The escapees left behind dummies in their beds to buy time before the prison guards discovered their absence. Despite an extensive manhunt and investigations by the FBI, the fate of the escapees remains unknown. The official conclusion is that they likely drowned in the treacherous waters of the bay. However, their bodies were never found, leading to persistent theories and speculation that they might have successfully made it to shore or even to freedom. The Alcatraz escape has become a legendary tale, leaving a lasting mystery about the ultimate fate of Frank Morris and the Anglin brothers.

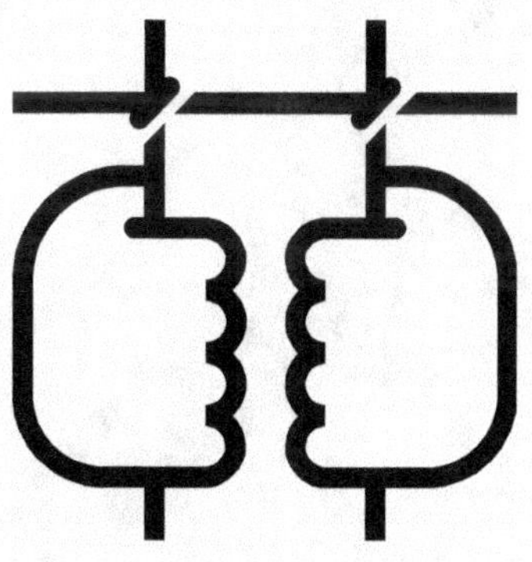

QUESTION 73

Why are There "Righties" and "Lefties"?

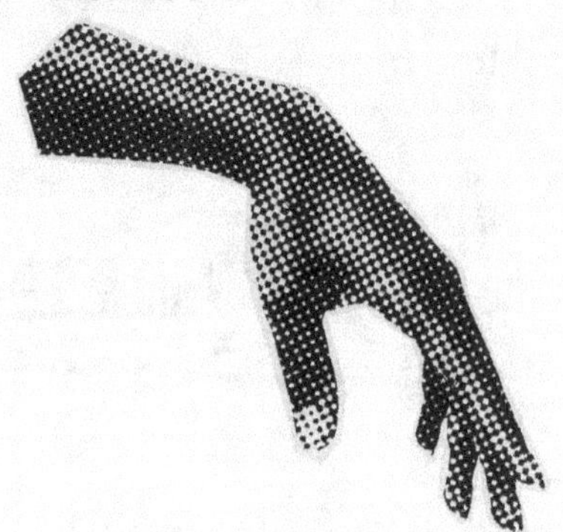

The mystery of why some people are "righties" (right-handed) and others are "lefties" (left-handed) is connected to how our brains are organized. The brain has two halves called hemispheres – the right hemisphere and the left hemisphere. Each hemisphere controls the opposite side of our body. So, if you're right-handed, it means the left hemisphere of your brain is more in charge of controlling your right hand.

For most people, the left hemisphere is the boss when it comes to language and fine motor skills like writing. That's why about 90% of the population is right-handed. It's just the way our brains are wired. On the flip side, left-handedness happens when the right hemisphere is more dominant for certain functions. Lefties make up a smaller percentage of the population, around 10%.

The reasons behind why someone becomes a righty or a lefty are still a bit of a puzzle. It seems to involve a mix of things like genetics, the environment we grow up in, and how our brains develop. Studying why people are right-handed or left-handed helps scientists unravel the fascinating complexity of our brains and how they control our movements and skills.

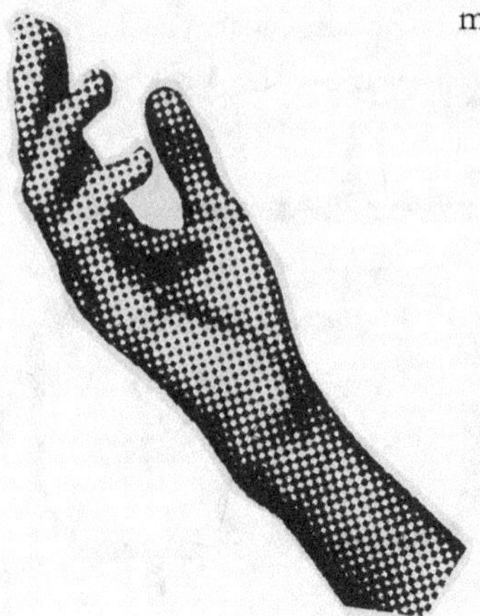

QUESTION 74

Why do we yawn?

Yawning is a natural and widespread behavior, but the exact reason why we yawn isn't completely understood. One common belief is that yawning helps increase the intake of oxygen and release of carbon dioxide. When we yawn, we take in a big breath, and the stretching of our jaw and face muscles may also increase blood flow, helping to wake us up and feel more alert.

Yawning can be contagious, meaning that when one person yawns, it might make others around them yawn too. This social aspect of yawning suggests that it might have a communicative function. In social groups, synchronized yawning could signal a shared state of relaxation or tiredness. It's like a way for our bodies to communicate non-verbally with others around us, almost like saying, "I'm feeling a bit sleepy, how about you?"

Interestingly, yawning doesn't just happen when we're tired or bored. It can occur for various reasons, including when we're anxious, anticipating something, or even when our brain needs a cool-down. While the precise reasons for yawning are still a bit of a mystery, scientists continue to explore the many facets of this seemingly simple yet fascinating behavior to uncover more about its functions and significance.

QUESTION 75

Why do we like music?

The love for music is deeply rooted in the way our brains are wired. When we listen to music, our brains release a chemical called dopamine, often referred to as the "feel-good" neurotransmitter. Dopamine is associated with pleasure and reward, and it plays a crucial role in the brain's reward system. This release of dopamine is a biological explanation for why we feel joy, excitement, or even relaxation when we listen to our favorite tunes..

While the broad understanding of why humans enjoy music involves factors like the release of dopamine and emotional connections, there are still aspects of our affinity for music that remain mysterious and continue to be explored.

One of the enduring mysteries is the universality of music appreciation across different cultures and societies. While the specific genres and styles of music may vary, the fundamental enjoyment of music appears to be a shared human experience. Researchers are intrigued by why certain patterns of sound, melody, and rhythm have such a widespread appeal and evoke similar emotional responses across diverse populations.

Additionally, the intricacies of individual preferences and why certain people are drawn to specific genres or musical elements over others pose interesting questions. The interplay between nature and nurture in shaping musical preferences, as well as the role of cultural influences, remains an area of ongoing investigation.

In essence, while we have a general understanding of the neurological and emotional aspects that contribute to our love for music, the finer details of why certain patterns are universally appealing and how individual preferences develop are aspects that scientists and scholars are still unraveling. The mystery of music appreciation adds an element of fascination to our complex relationship with this art form.

QUESTION 76

Can we unravel the mysteries behind the identity and motives of the infamous Zodiac Killer, who terrorized California in the late 1960s and early 1970s?

The identity and motives of the infamous Zodiac Killer, who struck fear into California during the late 1960s and early 1970s, remain one of the most enduring mysteries in criminal history. The Zodiac Killer is believed to be responsible for a series of unsolved murders and claimed to have committed more in encrypted letters sent to newspapers. The killer's cryptic codes and letters added an extra layer of mystery, leaving both investigators and the public perplexed.

Law enforcement and amateur sleuths have tried for decades to unravel the Zodiac Killer's identity, but the case remains unsolved. The killer cleverly avoided leaving behind definitive evidence at crime scenes, complicating the efforts to identify and apprehend them. The cryptograms sent by the Zodiac Killer also added a puzzling element, with some codes yet to be fully deciphered, adding to the mystique surrounding the case.

The motives behind the Zodiac Killer's actions remain unclear. The killer seemed to taunt the police and the public through cryptic messages, which fueled speculation about their psychological state and motivations. The fear and uncertainty created by the Zodiac Killer left a lasting impact on the collective consciousness, and despite decades of investigations and theories, the true identity and motives of this elusive criminal remain shrouded in mystery.

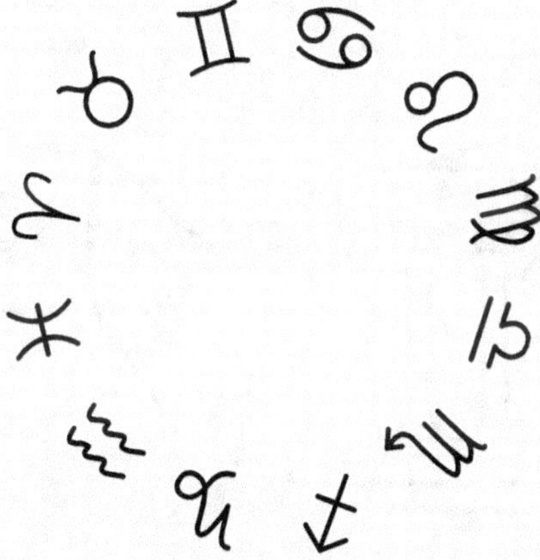

QUESTION 77

Can we uncover the true story behind the unsolved case of the Isabella Stewart Gardner Museum art heist, one of the largest thefts of cultural artifacts in history?

The Isabella Stewart Gardner Museum art heist is a captivating mystery that unfolded on March 18, 1990, in Boston, Massachusetts. Two thieves dressed as police officers entered the museum during the early hours and stole 13 pieces of art, including masterpieces by Vermeer, Rembrandt, and Manet. The stolen artworks had an estimated value of over $500 million, making it one of the largest and most notorious art thefts in history.

Despite decades of investigations and efforts, the true identity of the thieves and the whereabouts of the stolen art remain unknown. The thieves, cleverly avoiding the museum's advanced security system, left behind empty frames and a mystery that has puzzled law enforcement and art enthusiasts alike. The stolen pieces have not surfaced on the legitimate art market, suggesting the possibility that they are held privately or even destroyed.

The Isabella Stewart Gardner Museum continues to offer a substantial reward for information leading to the recovery of the stolen art, but the case remains unsolved. Theories abound, ranging from organized crime involvement to the possibility that the thieves were motivated by personal reasons. The lasting impact of this heist goes beyond the monetary value of the stolen artworks, leaving an indelible mark on the world of art and highlighting the challenges of recovering culturally significant pieces once they vanish into the shadows. The Gardner Museum heist stands as a symbol of the enduring mysteries that surround some of the world's greatest art crimes.

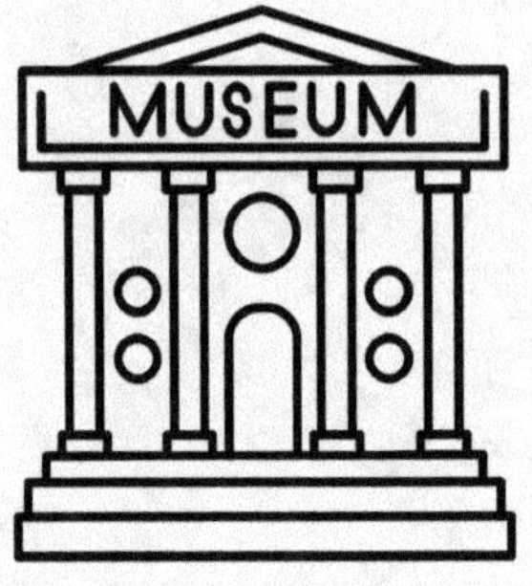

QUESTION 78

What were the motives and methods of famous bank robbers like Bonnie and Clyde, and how did their criminal exploits capture the public imagination?

Bonnie and Clyde, the infamous criminal duo from the Great Depression era, captivated the public through daring bank robberies, rebellion against authority, and a romanticized image fueled by media coverage. Motivated by economic hardship and a desire for an outlaw lifestyle, the couple's crime spree included audacious bank heists and shootouts with law enforcement across several states. Their ability to elude authorities added to their notoriety during a challenging period in American history. The public's fascination with Bonnie and Clyde was intensified by media portrayals that depicted them as glamorous antiheroes, creating a mythic image of a young, attractive couple living outside societal bounds. This romanticized view, coupled with economic struggles during the 1930s, garnered sympathy for the criminal duo. However, the story of Bonnie and Clyde, while well-documented, contains elements that remain mysterious and subject to interpretation.

The motivations behind their criminal activities, the dynamics of their partnership, and the enduring public fascination with their story involve complex psychological and sociological factors that continue to intrigue historians and criminologists. The blurred line between reality and myth, coupled with the challenges of understanding the intricacies of their mindset, adds layers of mystery to their narrative. Bonnie and Clyde remain legendary figures in American criminal history, symbolizing the intricate interplay between crime, media, and societal perceptions during a tumultuous period.

QUESTION 79

Why do we all have different fingerprints?

The uniqueness of fingerprints is a fascinating aspect of human biology that has intrigued scientists for centuries. Each person's fingerprints are distinct, even among identical twins. The story behind this lies in the development of fingerprints during fetal development. When a baby is in the womb, the ridges and valleys of their fingerprints form as a result of pressure on the skin caused by the surrounding amniotic fluid. This process, along with genetic factors, contributes to the individuality of fingerprints.

Fingerprints are made up of ridges and valleys, and the patterns they form fall into three main categories: arches, loops, and whorls. The specific arrangement of these patterns, as well as the minutiae points where ridges end or split, adds to the uniqueness of each person's fingerprints. Even though the basic patterns are shared among individuals, the combination and arrangement of these features make each fingerprint entirely distinctive.

Fingerprint analysis, known as dermatoglyphics, has been a crucial tool in forensic science for identifying individuals. The chances of two people having identical fingerprints are incredibly low, making fingerprints a reliable method for personal identification. The use of fingerprints in criminal investigations dates back to the late 19th century, and modern technology has further enhanced the precision and efficiency of fingerprint analysis.

While the exact reasons behind the uniqueness of fingerprints are not fully understood, it's believed to be a combination of genetic factors, environmental influences during fetal development, and the chaotic nature of ridge pattern formation. The intricate and individualized nature of fingerprints not only serves as a reliable method for identification but also adds a layer of wonder to the marvels of human biology.

QUESTION 80

Can we uncover the truth about the identity and motivations of the infamous Unabomber, Theodore Kaczynski, who carried out a nationwide bombing campaign?

The Unabomber, Theodore Kaczynski, perpetrated a nationwide bombing campaign that terrorized the United States for nearly two decades. Operating between 1978 and 1995, Kaczynski targeted individuals involved with modern technology and industrial society, sending homemade bombs through the mail. His actions resulted in three deaths and numerous injuries. The Unabomber became one of the FBI's most wanted criminals, and the case remained unsolved for years.

Kaczynski's motivations and identity were shrouded in mystery until 1996 when, in an unusual turn of events, he offered to stop the bombings if major newspapers published his manifesto, titled "Industrial Society and Its Future." In the manifesto, Kaczynski outlined his extreme anti-technology and anti-industrialization views, advocating for a return to a more primitive and nature-oriented way of life. The publication of the manifesto led to a tip from Kaczynski's brother, David, who recognized his writing style, ultimately leading to Theodore Kaczynski's arrest in 1996.

During his trial, Kaczynski pleaded guilty to all charges and was subsequently sentenced to life in prison without the possibility of parole. His case shed light on the challenges of balancing individual freedoms with the responsibilities of technological advancement. Kaczynski's extreme acts were driven by a fervent belief that modern technology posed an existential threat to humanity, and he saw his bombings as a desperate attempt to garner attention for his radical ideas.

The Unabomber case remains a significant chapter in criminal history, highlighting the complexities of understanding and addressing individuals who resort to violence in the pursuit of their ideologies. Kaczynski's story raises questions about the intersection of mental health, societal impact, and the consequences of extreme beliefs taken to violent extremes.

QUESTION 81

How did the Lindbergh baby kidnapping case in 1932 captivate the nation, and what were the investigative challenges and outcomes?

The Lindbergh baby kidnapping case in 1932 was a deeply captivating and tragic event that held the nation's attention. Charles Lindbergh Jr., the 20-month-old son of aviator Charles Lindbergh and his wife Anne, was kidnapped from their New Jersey home. The Lindberghs were an iconic couple, and the kidnapping of their young son shocked the nation. The case quickly became a media sensation, with newspapers providing extensive coverage of the unfolding drama.

The investigative challenges were significant, as law enforcement faced the daunting task of solving the first highly publicized kidnapping case in the United States. Despite paying a ransom, the Lindberghs' worst fears were realized when the baby's body was discovered not far from their home. The case marked the beginning of the Lindbergh Law, which made kidnapping a federal offense, reflecting the impact this high-profile crime had on the nation's legal landscape.

The investigation led to the arrest of Bruno Hauptmann, a German immigrant, who was found with a portion of the ransom money. Hauptmann's trial garnered intense public interest and was covered extensively by the media. Despite maintaining his innocence, Hauptmann was convicted and sentenced to death. The Lindbergh baby kidnapping case remains one of the most infamous criminal trials in American history. The tragedy had a lasting impact on the Lindbergh family, influencing their lives and contributing to changes in kidnapping laws to protect children in the future.

QUESTION 82

Who created Bitcoin?

Bitcoin, the first decentralized digital currency, was created by an individual or group using the pseudonym Satoshi Nakamoto. The story of Bitcoin's creation begins in 2008 when Nakamoto published a white paper titled "Bitcoin: A Peer-to-Peer Electronic Cash System." This document outlined the principles and mechanisms behind a new form of digital currency that would operate on a decentralized network using a technology called blockchain.

In January 2009, Nakamoto mined the first block of the Bitcoin blockchain, known as the "genesis block," and embedded a message referencing a headline from that day to establish a historical timestamp. This marked the birth of Bitcoin as a functional and operational cryptocurrency. Nakamoto continued to be involved in the development and expansion of the Bitcoin network, collaborating with other early adopters and contributors.

Despite the significant impact of Bitcoin on the financial and technological landscape, Satoshi Nakamoto's true identity remains unknown. Nakamoto communicated with the Bitcoin community through online forums and email but gradually faded from public view. In 2011, Nakamoto handed over control of the Bitcoin code repository and network alert key to a group of developers, making the project more decentralized.

The mystery surrounding Nakamoto's identity has led to various speculations, but the creator's anonymity has been maintained. The legacy of Bitcoin is not only in its innovative technology but also in how it has revolutionized the concept of decentralized, peer-to-peer digital currencies, opening up new possibilities for financial transactions and challenging traditional monetary systems.

QUESTION 83

Can we unravel the mysteries surrounding historical disappearances, such as the vanishing of aviation pioneer Amelia Earhart?

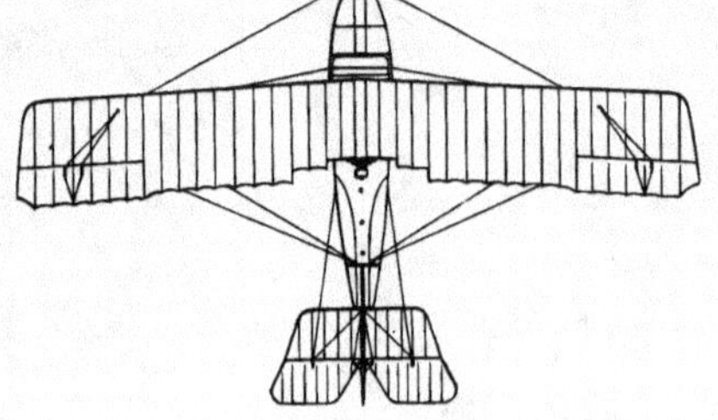

The disappearance of aviation pioneer Amelia Earhart in 1937 remains one of the greatest mysteries in history. Earhart was attempting to circumnavigate the globe when her plane disappeared over the Pacific Ocean. The story begins on July 2, 1937, when Earhart and her navigator, Fred Noonan, took off from Papua New Guinea for Howland Island. Unfortunately, they never arrived, and their disappearance sparked numerous theories and searches.

The primary challenge in unraveling the mystery lies in the vastness of the Pacific Ocean, where the plane is believed to have gone down. Despite extensive search efforts at the time, no trace of Earhart, Noonan, or their plane was found. Over the years, various theories emerged, ranging from crash and sinking to the possibility of Earhart and Noonan surviving and being captured by the Japanese.

In recent years, technological advancements and underwater exploration have led to renewed efforts to locate Earhart's plane. Expedition teams have used sonar and remotely operated vehicles to search the ocean floor near Howland Island. While some artifacts were discovered, definitive evidence linking them to Earhart's plane has been elusive, leaving the mystery largely unsolved.

The disappearance of Amelia Earhart continues to captivate the public's imagination, and various expeditions and research initiatives persist in the quest to uncover the truth behind her vanishing. The mystery endures, leaving room for speculation and intrigue about the fate of one of aviation's most iconic figures.

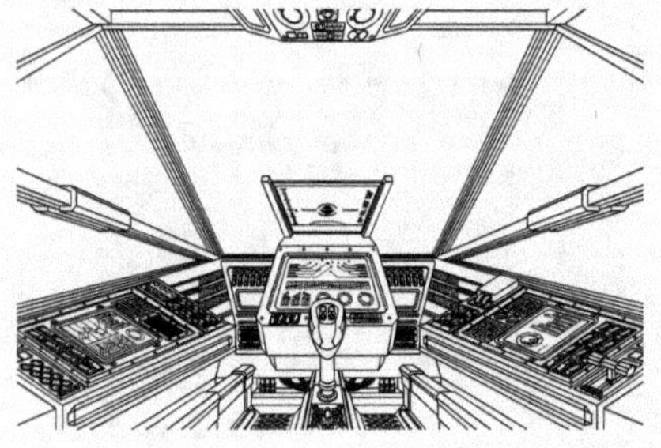

QUESTION 84

Can we unravel the mysteries of animal communication, including the intricate languages of whales, birdsong, and the complex signaling of primates?

Unraveling the mysteries of animal communication involves delving into the intricate languages of various species, from the haunting songs of whales to the melodious birdsong and the complex signaling of primates. The story of this exploration begins with scientists aiming to decode the ways animals convey information, emotions, and even cultural nuances.

Whales, particularly humpback whales, are known for their mesmerizing songs. These complex vocalizations, often referred to as whale songs, are not random; they follow patterns and structures. Scientists have been studying these songs to understand their purpose, discovering that they are likely related to mating rituals and navigation. The mysteries lie in deciphering the specific meanings behind different components of the songs and how they contribute to social interactions within whale communities.

Birdsong, another fascinating realm of animal communication, involves the intricate melodies and patterns produced by various bird species. Birds use songs for diverse purposes, including marking territory, attracting mates, and communicating with their young. The story of unraveling this mystery involves ornithologists and ethologists meticulously analyzing different bird species' songs to discern their functions, variations, and the cultural transmission of specific tunes within bird communities.

Primates, our closest relatives in the animal kingdom, communicate through a complex system of vocalizations, gestures, and facial expressions. The story of understanding primate communication involves observing their behaviors in the wild and in captivity. Researchers have identified specific calls for different circumstances, such as alarm calls indicating the presence of predators or distinctive vocalizations during social interactions. Deciphering the subtleties of primate communication also involves recognizing the importance of body language and facial expressions in conveying emotional states and maintaining social cohesion.

Advancements in technology, including high-tech recording devices and sophisticated analytical tools, have significantly contributed to unraveling these mysteries. As scientists continue their research, the goal is to not only decode the basic meanings behind animal signals but also to appreciate the richness and complexity of their communication systems. Ultimately, this exploration enhances our understanding of the diverse ways in which animals convey information and reinforces the importance of preserving their natural habitats for the continuation of these intricate languages.

QUESTION 85

Can we uncover the secrets of animal navigation, from the precision of homing pigeons to the incredible journeys of sea turtles across vast ocean distances?

The exploration of animal navigation has been a captivating story of uncovering the secrets behind the precision of homing pigeons and the incredible journeys of sea turtles. Homing pigeons, also known as messenger pigeons, have been remarkable companions to humans for centuries. The mystery lies in how these birds can accurately find their way back to their home lofts over long distances. Researchers have discovered that homing pigeons use a combination of visual, magnetic, and olfactory cues. They rely on landmarks, the Earth's magnetic field, and even the sense of smell to navigate, showcasing a multi-faceted approach to finding their way home. Sea turtles, on the other hand, embark on epic journeys across vast ocean distances, navigating through open waters with astonishing precision. The story of sea turtle navigation involves a combination of instinct and environmental cues. Scientists believe that sea turtles use Earth's magnetic field as a guide, allowing them to navigate across thousands of miles during migrations. Additionally, they may rely on the Earth's gravitational field, the position of the sun, and the temperature of the water to orient themselves. These long-distance journeys, such as the ones undertaken by loggerhead or leatherback sea turtles, remain a testament to the incredible navigational abilities embedded in these ancient travelers.

The research on animal navigation not only unveils the marvels of their innate abilities but also serves as inspiration for human technology. Studying the mechanisms animals use for navigation has influenced the development of navigation systems, such as GPS, that we use in our daily lives. By understanding and appreciating the intricacies of animal navigation, scientists aim to gain insights into both the natural world and potential applications that can benefit human endeavors.

QUESTION 86

How do animals, such as bees and ants, display collective intelligence and cooperative behavior in their colonies?

The collective intelligence and cooperative behavior observed in animal colonies, particularly among bees and ants, form a fascinating story of intricate social structures. These colonies operate as highly organized communities where individuals work together for the benefit of the entire group. Bees and ants showcase a remarkable division of labor, with each member having a specific role to play in tasks like foraging, nursing, and defending the colony. The mystery lies in how these individuals coordinate their actions seamlessly, responding to changing conditions and contributing to the overall success of the colony.

Communication is a key element in the story of collective intelligence. Bees, for instance, communicate through intricate dances that convey information about the location of food sources. Ants use pheromones, chemical signals, to leave trails that guide others to resources or warn them of potential threats. The mysteries in these communication systems revolve around the depth of understanding among colony members and how information is shared to optimize the collective decision-making process. Scientists are still unraveling the nuances of these communication methods and their role in maintaining the cohesion of the colony.

The evolution of these behaviors raises questions about the mysteries of how such complex systems emerged and how they continue to adapt. The story of collective intelligence in bee and ant colonies involves not only the fascinating behaviors observed today but also the evolutionary processes that led to the development of these social structures. Exploring these mysteries contributes not only to our understanding of these remarkable insects but also to insights that may have applications in fields like robotics and artificial intelligence, where the principles of collective intelligence are increasingly being explored and implemented.

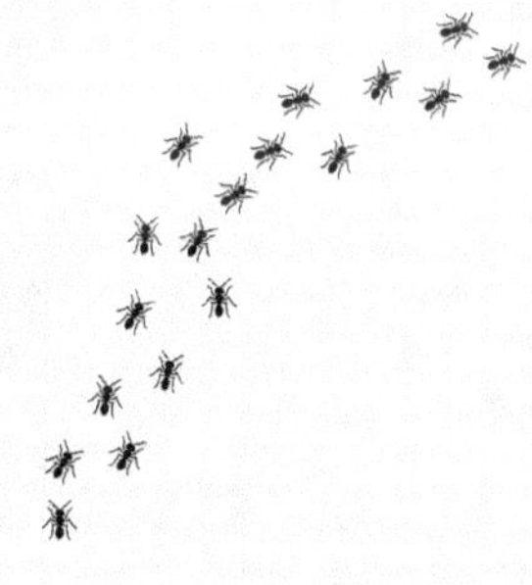

QUESTION 87

How many perfect numbers exist, and can we determine if an odd perfect number exists?

Perfect numbers are a unique concept in mathematics, and the story of their exploration has been ongoing for centuries. A perfect number is a positive integer that is equal to the sum of its proper divisors, excluding itself. The search for perfect numbers began in ancient times, with the discovery of the first perfect number, 6, by the Greeks. They found that 6 can be divided by 1, 2, and 3, and the sum of these divisors equals 6.

The mystery of perfect numbers lies in determining how many of them exist and whether odd perfect numbers are possible. As of now, all known perfect numbers are even, and a comprehensive understanding of odd perfect numbers remains elusive. Mathematicians have been exploring the properties and patterns of perfect numbers through various mathematical techniques and algorithms. The search for odd perfect numbers involves intricate computations and examinations of number theory, with researchers looking for patterns that might reveal the existence or non-existence of odd perfect numbers.

The quest for perfect numbers is not only a mathematical puzzle but also a journey into the depths of number theory. While the existence of odd perfect numbers remains uncertain, mathematicians continue to develop new methods and refine existing ones in the pursuit of understanding the mysteries surrounding perfect numbers and expanding our knowledge of the intricate world of mathematics.

QUESTION 88

What is the fundamental cause of the mysterious behavior of soap bubbles, and can we create a comprehensive mathematical model that describes their shapes?

The behavior of soap bubbles is a captivating story that intertwines physics, chemistry, and mathematics. The fundamental cause of their mysterious behavior lies in the delicate balance between surface tension and pressure. Surface tension is the tendency of a liquid surface to minimize its area, essentially pulling the bubble into a spherical shape. At the same time, the pressure inside the bubble, caused by the air trapped within, pushes outward, resisting the natural tendency of the surface tension to contract. This delicate interplay results in the formation of the thin film we see as a soap bubble.

The story of understanding soap bubbles involves the exploration of mathematical models that describe their shapes. Mathematicians and physicists have sought to create comprehensive models that predict the intricate patterns and colors observed in soap bubbles. The mathematical equations involved are based on the minimization of surface area subject to constraints, taking into account the effects of gravity, air pressure, and the interactions between neighboring bubbles. This quest for mathematical precision is an ongoing journey, and scientists continue to refine their models to capture the full complexity of soap bubble behavior.

While the shapes of soap bubbles may appear simple, the underlying mathematics is surprisingly rich and nuanced. The story of works on soap bubbles involves not only the development of mathematical models but also the application of these models to real-world scenarios, from artistic creations to industrial processes. Understanding the mathematics of soap bubbles not only adds a layer of fascination to their whimsical appearance but also provides valuable insights into the fundamental principles governing the behavior of fluids at the microscopic level.

QUESTION 89

Can we uncover the mathematical principles governing the patterns observed in natural phenomena, such as the arrangements of petals in a flower or the distribution of leaves on a stem?

The exploration of mathematical principles governing patterns in nature, known as phyllotaxis, is a captivating story that involves uncovering the hidden order behind the arrangements of petals, leaves, or other plant structures. The study of phyllotaxis dates back centuries, with scientists and mathematicians fascinated by the seemingly regular and intricate patterns observed in various plant formations. One of the key figures in this story is mathematician and scientist D'Arcy Wentworth Thompson, who made significant contributions to understanding the mathematical relationships in biological forms.

The story of the works on phyllotaxis delves into the development of mathematical models that describe the observed patterns. One notable model involves the concept of spiral phyllotaxis, where plant structures follow a spiral pattern around a central axis. The Fibonacci sequence, a series of numbers where each number is the sum of the two preceding ones, frequently appears in these spiral arrangements. The golden ratio, another mathematical concept, also plays a role in describing the optimal angles between plant structures. The application of these mathematical principles helps unravel the underlying order in seemingly complex natural patterns.

The quest to uncover mathematical principles in phyllotaxis continues with the collaboration of biologists, mathematicians, and physicists. The story involves not only the development of mathematical models but also experimental observations and advancements in imaging technology that allow scientists to study these patterns at a finer scale. By deciphering the mathematical rules governing phyllotaxis, researchers aim to gain insights into the fundamental processes shaping the diversity and beauty of plant structures, demonstrating the intimate connection between mathematics and the intricacies of the natural world.

QUESTION 90

What is the presence and origin of symmetry in the world?

Symmetry is a fascinating and universal concept that spans various disciplines, including mathematics, physics, biology, and art. It involves identifying patterns or structures that remain unchanged under specific transformations, with reflection symmetry being a fundamental type where an object looks the same when reflected along a line. Mathematicians, drawing on tools like group theory, have classified symmetrical patterns, finding applications in crystals, the natural world, and even the laws of physics.

The story of symmetry extends to art, where artists utilize mathematical principles to create visually pleasing compositions. The universality of symmetry across different fields highlights its essential role in the structure and beauty of the world. However, the mystery of symmetry lies in its pervasive nature and the intricate connections between mathematical principles and natural patterns. The unanswered question of why symmetry is so prevalent in the universe adds to its mysterious allure. Additionally, the subjective and cultural aspects of symmetry in art, including preferences and aesthetic appeal, contribute to the ongoing mystery. In essence, symmetry's ability to transcend disciplines and shape both the fundamental structures of the universe and our aesthetic perceptions keeps its mystery alive in the pursuit of knowledge.

QUESTION 91

What is the definitive cause of migraine headaches, and can we develop a foolproof method for their prevention and treatment?

The definitive cause of migraine headaches is a complex puzzle that scientists and researchers have been working to unravel. Migraines are believed to involve a combination of genetic, environmental, and neurological factors. One key element is the role of blood vessels and the nervous system. During a migraine, blood vessels in the brain may constrict and then dilate, leading to a cascade of events that result in pain and other symptoms. The release of certain chemicals, such as serotonin, also plays a role in this process.

The story of understanding migraines involves a deep dive into the intricate workings of the brain and the nervous system. Researchers have conducted studies to identify specific triggers for migraines, such as certain foods, stress, hormonal changes, or environmental factors. Advances in brain imaging techniques have allowed scientists to observe the changes in the brain during a migraine attack. However, the precise mechanism and the interplay of various factors remain areas of ongoing research. Developing a foolproof method for the prevention and treatment of migraines is a challenging but active area of investigation. Medications, lifestyle changes, and therapies are currently used to manage migraines, but a one-size-fits-all solution has proven elusive. Tailoring treatments based on individual factors and gaining a deeper understanding of the intricate processes involved in migraines are essential steps toward more effective prevention and relief. The story of migraine research is one of ongoing discovery, bringing hope for improved strategies to alleviate the impact of these debilitating headaches on individuals' lives.

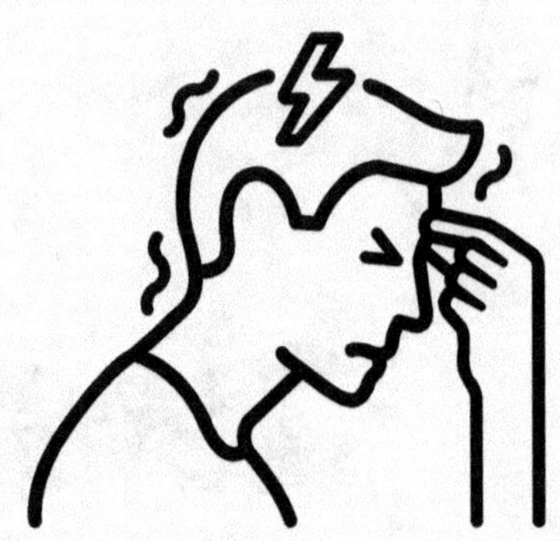

QUESTION 92

What causes aging at the cellular and molecular levels, and can we discover interventions to slow down or reverse the aging process?

The aging process at the cellular and molecular levels is a multifaceted story that scientists are diligently unraveling. At the cellular level, one prominent factor is the shortening of telomeres, which are protective caps at the ends of chromosomes. Telomeres naturally shorten with each cell division, eventually reaching a point where cells can no longer replicate, leading to aging. Additionally, cellular damage accumulates over time due to various factors such as environmental stress, toxins, and metabolic processes.

Researchers are delving into the intricate mechanisms that drive aging, exploring the role of genes, cellular communication, and the impact of free radicals. The study of senescence, a state in which cells cease to divide, has gained prominence in understanding aging. Senescent cells can accumulate in tissues, contributing to age-related diseases and impairing organ function. Scientists are working to decipher the signaling pathways and molecular changes involved in this process.

While the prospect of fully reversing aging remains a formidable challenge, the field of longevity research is actively seeking interventions to slow down the aging process. Caloric restriction, genetic manipulations in model organisms, and pharmaceutical interventions are areas of exploration. Researchers are also investigating the potential of enhancing cellular repair mechanisms and targeting specific pathways involved in aging. The story of anti-aging interventions is a dynamic narrative, driven by a quest to extend healthy lifespans and mitigate the impact of age-related diseases on human health.

QUESTION 93

How do hiccups occur, and can we find a foolproof method to stop them without relying on traditional remedies?

Hiccups are involuntary contractions of the diaphragm, the muscle that separates the chest from the abdomen and plays a crucial role in breathing. The diaphragm suddenly contracts, causing a quick closure of the vocal cords, which produces the characteristic "hic" sound. While hiccups are a common and usually harmless occurrence, the exact triggers can vary, ranging from eating too quickly to consuming carbonated beverages or experiencing sudden temperature changes.

The story of hiccups involves the complex coordination of the diaphragm, nerves, and the respiratory system. Normally, the diaphragm contracts rhythmically, allowing us to breathe smoothly. However, when the diaphragm contracts involuntarily, hiccups occur. This can be triggered by various factors that irritate the nerves controlling the diaphragm. While most hiccups resolve on their own and are not a cause for concern, persistent hiccups lasting more than 48 hours may warrant medical attention.

Despite the plethora of traditional remedies for stopping hiccups, finding a foolproof method can be elusive. Common remedies include holding one's breath, drinking a glass of water quickly, or having someone startle you. The effectiveness of these methods varies, and what works for one person may not work for another. Researchers continue to explore novel approaches to halt hiccups, but a universally foolproof method remains an intriguing challenge in the medical world.

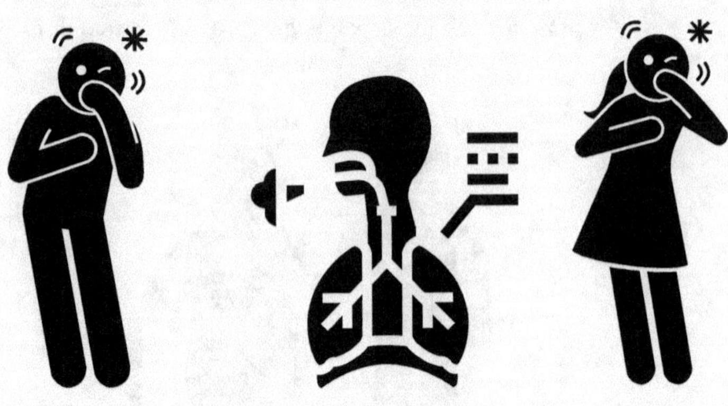

QUESTION 94

Why do we experience "butterflies in the stomach" during moments of stress or excitement, and what physiological processes contribute to this sensation?

The sensation of "butterflies in the stomach" during moments of stress or excitement is a result of the intricate interplay between the brain and the gut. The gut and the brain are connected through a complex network known as the gut-brain axis. When we encounter a stressful or exciting situation, the brain signals the release of stress hormones, including adrenaline, as part of the "fight or flight" response. These stress hormones affect various systems in the body, including the digestive system.

In response to stress hormones, blood is redirected away from the digestive organs, including the stomach, and towards the muscles to prepare the body for quick action. The physiological changes in blood flow and the release of stress hormones can lead to a fluttery or nervous feeling in the stomach. Additionally, the gut contains a vast network of neurons known as the enteric nervous system, often referred to as the "second brain." This system can respond to emotional stimuli independently of the central nervous system, contributing to the sensation of butterflies.

The story of "butterflies in the stomach" is a fascinating illustration of the mind-body connection. The emotional and psychological experiences we undergo can have tangible effects on the physical sensations in our gut. Understanding this intricate relationship sheds light on how our bodies respond to different emotional states and provides insight into the holistic nature of human experience. The mystery lies in the nuanced connection between our emotions and physical sensations, particularly the fluttery feeling in the stomach during moments of stress or excitement. While science offers explanations for the physiological processes involved, the intricacies of how our emotions manifest in specific bodily sensations remain a captivating mystery. Delving into the mysteries of the mind-body connection and the ways our emotional states influence our physical experiences is an ongoing journey, offering both scientific exploration and a touch of enigma in understanding the complexities of human nature.

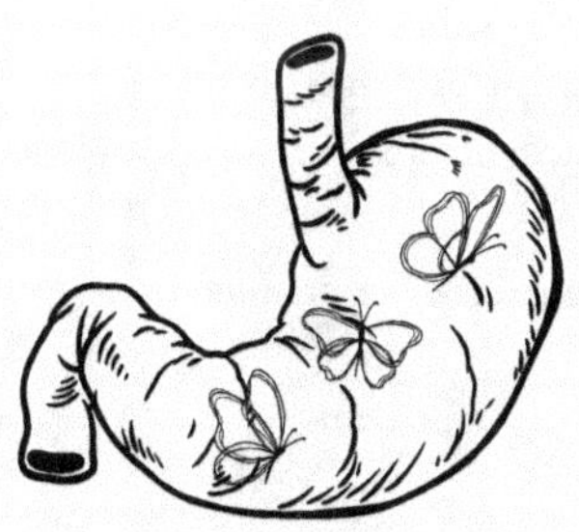

QUESTION 95

Can we definitively solve the mystery of the "Black Dahlia" murder, a brutal and unsolved killing of aspiring actress Elizabeth Short in 1947, and uncover the identity of her murderer?

The "Black Dahlia" murder is one of the most infamous and enduring mysteries in true crime history, marked by the brutal and unsolved killing of Elizabeth Short in 1947. The story begins with the discovery of Short's mutilated body in a vacant lot in Los Angeles, sparking widespread media coverage and public fascination. Short, an aspiring actress, was nicknamed the "Black Dahlia" by the press due to her penchant for wearing black clothing.

The mystery surrounding the Black Dahlia murder lies in the lack of a definitive resolution despite intense investigations and public attention. Elizabeth Short's murder remains unsolved, with multiple theories and suspects proposed over the years. The gruesome nature of the crime, coupled with the compelling details of Short's life, has contributed to the enduring fascination with this case. The story is shrouded in speculation and unanswered questions, as investigators and amateur sleuths alike continue to delve into the evidence, seeking to uncover the truth behind the identity of Short's murderer.

The enduring enigma of the Black Dahlia murder persists not only because of the gruesomeness of the crime but also due to the lack of closure and the myriad theories surrounding the case. The mystery captivates true crime enthusiasts, historians, and the public alike, prompting ongoing investigations and discussions about who may have been responsible for Elizabeth Short's tragic and untimely demise. Despite the passage of decades, the quest to solve the Black Dahlia mystery remains active, symbolizing the enduring allure of unsolved crimes in the annals of criminal history.

QUESTION 96

Is there a definitive answer to why we find certain foods more appetizing than others, and can we uncover the precise interplay of factors influencing taste preferences?

The appeal of certain foods over others is a captivating story shaped by a combination of biological, psychological, and cultural factors. At the biological level, our taste preferences are influenced by our evolutionary history. For example, humans have evolved to favor foods that are rich in energy and nutrients, such as those containing sugars and fats, as a survival mechanism. This inherent preference for certain tastes is deeply rooted in our genetic makeup.

Beyond biology, psychological factors play a crucial role in shaping our taste preferences. Individual experiences, memories, and cultural influences contribute to the development of our unique palate. Early exposure to certain flavors during childhood can create lasting preferences, and cultural practices and traditions also play a significant role in determining what foods we find appealing. The brain's reward system reinforces positive experiences with food, creating a connection between pleasure and specific tastes, further influencing our preferences.

The story of taste preferences is not only a blend of biology and psychology but also a reflection of societal and cultural dynamics. Food choices are embedded in the fabric of our communities and are often intertwined with traditions, rituals, and social gatherings. The interplay of these multifaceted factors creates a rich and complex narrative, making the study of taste preferences a fascinating exploration into the intricacies of human behavior and culture.

QUESTION 97

What causes the mysterious phenomenon of "brain freeze" when consuming cold substances, and can we develop strategies to prevent or alleviate this sensation?

The mysterious phenomenon known as "brain freeze" occurs when we consume something extremely cold, like ice cream or a frozen beverage, and experience a sudden, sharp headache. The story behind brain freeze involves the rapid cooling of the blood vessels at the back of the throat. When something cold touches the roof of the mouth (palate), it causes the blood vessels in that area to constrict and then rapidly dilate. This rapid change in blood flow triggers pain receptors, leading to the sensation of a headache or "brain freeze."

The mechanism behind brain freeze is akin to the body's response to cold temperatures. When we encounter extreme cold, the blood vessels in our skin constrict to conserve heat. However, when we consume something cold, this response occurs in the palate's blood vessels. While the headache is not directly related to the brain, the pain receptors in the mouth and face send signals to the brain, creating the sensation of pain.

While brain freeze is temporary and generally harmless, there are a few strategies to prevent or alleviate the sensation. Slowing down the consumption of cold substances can help minimize the sudden temperature change in the palate. Additionally, pressing the tongue or the thumb against the roof of the mouth can warm the area and potentially alleviate the discomfort. Understanding the simple yet fascinating science behind brain freeze provides insights into how our bodies respond to temperature stimuli and how we can navigate this quirky aspect of enjoying cold treats.

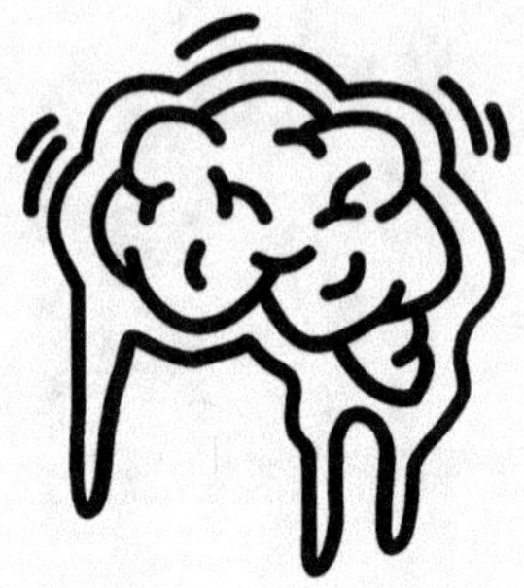

QUESTION 98

What causes the occasional involuntary muscle twitch or "eyelid twitch," and can we determine the factors influencing its occurrence?

The occasional muscle twitch, commonly experienced as an "eyelid twitch," is typically a harmless and spontaneous contraction of the muscles. The story behind these twitches involves the complex interplay of various factors. One primary factor is stress or fatigue. When our bodies are stressed or fatigued, the nervous system can become more excitable, leading to muscle contractions or twitches. Lack of sleep, excessive caffeine intake, and eye strain from staring at screens can contribute to this heightened excitability.

Another factor influencing muscle twitches is dehydration. When the body lacks proper hydration, the balance of electrolytes, essential for muscle function, can be disrupted. This imbalance may result in spontaneous muscle contractions, including those that cause eyelid twitches. Additionally, certain lifestyle factors, such as consuming excessive amounts of caffeine or alcohol, can contribute to muscle twitching.

While occasional muscle twitches are usually benign, persistent or severe twitching may warrant medical attention. It's essential to stay hydrated, manage stress, and ensure proper sleep to minimize the occurrence of these muscle twitches. Understanding the story behind these twitches sheds light on how lifestyle factors and the body's response mechanisms can influence our muscle functions.

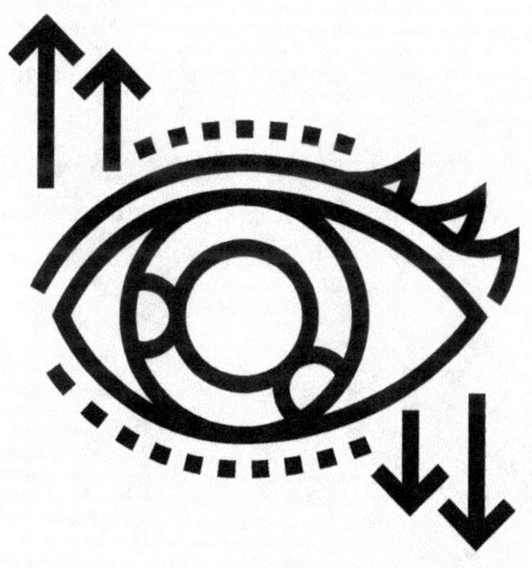

QUESTION 99

Can we explain the exact reasons behind the occasional ringing or buzzing in the ears, known as tinnitus, and find effective methods to alleviate or prevent it?

The occasional ringing or buzzing in the ears, known as tinnitus, has a story that involves various factors contributing to this auditory sensation. Tinnitus is often associated with damage to the hair cells in the inner ear. These hair cells play a crucial role in converting sound vibrations into electrical signals that the brain interprets as sound. When these cells are damaged, they can send signals to the brain that are perceived as a ringing or buzzing sound, even when there is no external source of the noise.

Exposure to loud noises is a common cause of tinnitus. Prolonged exposure to loud sounds, such as loud music, machinery noise, or frequent use of headphones at high volumes, can lead to damage of the delicate hair cells in the inner ear. In addition to noise-induced tinnitus, other factors like age-related hearing loss, earwax blockage, or certain medications can contribute to the development of tinnitus.

While there is no cure for tinnitus, various strategies can help alleviate or manage the symptoms. Protecting the ears from loud noises, managing stress, and avoiding excessive use of earbuds at high volumes are preventive measures. Sound therapy, cognitive behavioral therapy, and relaxation techniques are among the approaches used to help individuals cope with tinnitus. Understanding the multifaceted story of tinnitus involves recognizing the role of both external factors and internal mechanisms in creating this auditory sensation and exploring ways to mitigate its impact on daily life.

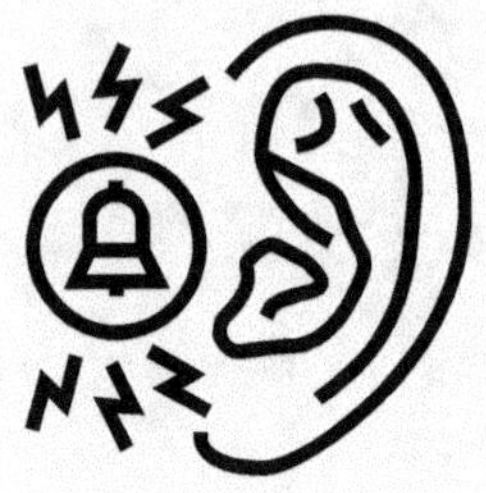

QUESTION 100

How does a cat always land on its feet when falling, and can we unveil the specific mechanisms that enable this uncanny feline ability?

The fascinating ability of cats to consistently land on their feet when falling is a result of a combination of instinctual behaviors and unique anatomical features. This remarkable skill is facilitated by the cat's extraordinary sense of balance and agility, made possible by a highly flexible spine and the absence of a collarbone. The "cat righting reflex," an instinct developed from a young age, involves the cat's inner ear, which detects changes in position and movement. This reflex triggers rapid twisting and turning to enable the cat to land on its feet during a fall.

An additional aspect of this acrobatic feat is the use of the tail as a counterbalance. The tail helps the cat control its descent, allowing for adjustments in position and maintaining stability. While scientists have made strides in understanding various components of this phenomenon, mysteries remain regarding the precise neural mechanisms involved and how the instinct evolves throughout a cat's life. The interplay between tail movements and body positioning adds complexity to the mystery, sparking curiosity about the detailed workings of this feline adaptation.

Beyond the intriguing nature of this behavior, the practical implications of understanding a cat's ability to right itself extend to potential applications in fields like robotics and biomechanics. Unraveling the mystery of how cats consistently land on their feet not only sheds light on the adaptations of these agile animals but also inspires broader inquiries into animal physiology and the intricate intersection of instinct and adaptation.

QUESTION 101

Can we definitively understand the reasons behind déjà vu, unraveling the cognitive and neurological processes that lead to the sensation of reliving a moment?

Déjà vu, the eerie feeling of experiencing something as if it has happened before, has intrigued researchers, but a definitive understanding remains elusive. Cognitive and neurological processes contribute to this phenomenon. One prevalent theory suggests that déjà vu occurs when there is a mismatch between the sensory input and the brain's memory retrieval process. In simpler terms, the brain may falsely recognize a current situation as a stored memory, leading to the sense of familiarity.

The hippocampus, a brain region crucial for memory formation, retrieval, and association, is often implicated in déjà vu. When the brain encounters a new situation that bears similarities to past experiences, the hippocampus may activate related memories, creating the feeling of déjà vu. However, the exact mechanisms and conditions triggering this process are complex and not fully understood. Additionally, research indicates that déjà vu is more common in young adults and may decrease with age. This observation hints at the role of brain maturation and the development of memory processes in the occurrence of déjà vu. While scientists have made progress in identifying potential factors, the precise interplay of cognitive and neurological elements contributing to déjà vu remains a captivating mystery in the exploration of human consciousness and memory.

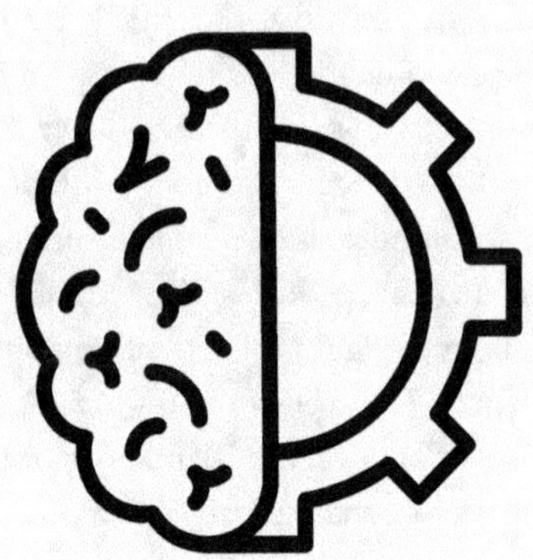

THE END